KIDS of the BLACK HOLE

KIDS of the BLACK HOLE

PUNK ROCK in Postsuburban California

Dewar MacLeod

UNIVERSITY OF OKLAHOMA PRESS : NORMAN

Pages ii–iii: Detail of photograph (See p. 84) of Darby Crash (Jan Pau Beahm, aka Bobby Pyn).
© Jenny Lens Punk Archive / Cache Agency

Library of Congress Cataloging-in-Publication Data
MacLeod, Dewar, 1962–
Kids of the black hole : punk rock in postsuburban California / Dewar MacLeod.
    p.   cm.
 ncludes bibliographical references and index.
ISBN 978-0-8061-4041-4 (hardcover : alk. paper)
1. Punk rock music—California—History and criticism.
I. Title.
ML3534.M305 2010
781.66—dc22
2010015042

The paper in this book meets the guidelines for permanence and durability of the Committee on Production Guidelines for Book Longevity of the Council on Library Resources, Inc. ∞

1 2 3 4 5 6 7 8 9 10

For Deirdre

Contents

Illustrations

INTRODUCTION

"Yep, Sid lives all right, and he's now got himself a tan."

Kickboy Face, 1980

In 1977, punk rock, the music and style of the working class and disen-franchised, surfaced in Los Angeles, the heartland of swimming pools, smog, and the American Dream. Kids taped trash bags on their bodies, tore and safety-pinned their T-shirts, spiked their hair, picked up guitars (even if they couldn't play), and formed bands. Within a few years punk spread from the bohemian enclave of Hollywood to the suburban tracts diffusing mile after mile across the Southern California landscape. White kids in Fullerton, Huntington Beach, Encino, and beyond shaved their hair into Mohawks, donned combat boots and spiked leather wristbands, and slammed into each other with fists, elbows, and bodies while "hard-core" punk bands raged from the stages about the false promises of mom, apple pie, and Ronald Reagan.

The story of what these young people were doing in the late 1970s and early 1980s is, first, an episode in the history of pop music. The punk rock of So Cal deserves its own place in the history of rock 'n' roll, even if, as one author perceived, "There has always been a surplus of lousy 'rock' bands, but hardcore was perhaps the first time on the planet that there was a fad for them."[1] So Cal punk was also an episode in the history of the culture industries and their critics. Finally, So Cal punk was an episode in the history of youth and leisure culture and more generally of urban/sub-urban/postsuburban geography and social formation.

Three historical currents of the postwar period—suburbia, youth culture, and mass culture—changed dramatically in the decade of the 1970s. The significant transformations of the seventies are quite clear from the perspective of the early twenty-first century. Urban geographers have described the growth of a new social formation, postsuburbia. Popular critics endlessly comment on the transformation of adolescence and youth culture with the arrival of Generations X, Y, E, and, the latest (as sung by the AKAs), "Generation Vexed." And scholars have documented the "end of mass culture." *Kids of the Black Hole* details a significant moment in the histories of these three related postwar developments by examining a phenomenon that seemed at the time to be sudden and inexplicable—the explosion of punk rock in seemingly placid suburbs in Southern California (and later throughout the country).

Punk rock developed as a musical form and performance style in the mid-1970s in New York City and became a major social phenomenon in 1976–77 with the formation of the Sex Pistols and a whole new punk subculture in London. Punk rock attempted to destroy rock 'n' roll from within, by reducing it to its most basic formulations. The archetypal punk band, New York's Ramones, played the simplest of rock 'n' roll: thumping $4/4$ beats, buzzsaw guitars without any leads, and a submerged, melodic pop hook.[2] Punk's loud, edgy, aggressive sound and its defiant, often angry lyrics were a revelation for those who were tired of the bland music that had replaced the innovative music of the 1960s. Its blunt antiauthoritarian message appealed especially to white English working-class youth, providing them with an outlet for the anger and alienation they were feeling about their place and their future in the crumbling British state.

When punk rock first emerged in Southern California, the developing scene self-consciously echoed and mimicked its predecessors in New York and London. Combining the poetics, artiness, showbiz cool, and goofy naughtiness of the New York bands with the theatricality, rebel politics, and anarchic rage of the British punks, a small group of artists, musicians, and ne'er-do-wells gathered together in Hollywood and called themselves punks in 1977. In the beginning punk in Los Angeles was mostly an aesthetic, a set of artistic creations. Punk rock music in Hollywood developed largely in response to, in dialogue with, the artistic and musical history of rock 'n' roll, and, specifically, the international music business centered in Los Angeles. Punk took hold in Hollywood initially as a musical-artistic response to perceived musical-artistic deadness.

Certainly, there were social issues involved as well, as punks encountered the world around them, but most punks mainly cared about the music and the music scene.

Around 1980 punk scenes blossomed in communities throughout the area surrounding Los Angeles. The new punk—a mutant offspring called "hardcore"—transformed the aesthetic, making both the music and the fashion harsher, more severe, less ironic. But it was not only an aesthetic development that occurred with hardcore. In fact, this book argues, the arrival of hardcore punk reflected transformations in both the position of young people in American society and the landscape of Southern California. Hardcore punk developed less out of musical circumstances than social ones.

The emergence of hardcore occurred first in the suburban towns of the Valleys and the South Bay area in Los Angeles County and in the coastal and nearby towns of Orange County, California. Hardcore took the stripped-down music of punk and stripped it down further. Hardcore was even faster and louder than punk, with songs often no more than a minute long. Setting its protest solidly in American suburbia, hardcore removed the urban working-class and artistic connotations from punk. While suburbia had always been essential to punk, as the place to leave and destroy, now suburbia was subject to assault from within. Bands such as Black Flag and the Middle Class did not abandon their suburban neighborhoods; they and other punks fostered local music scenes. Young, mostly white and male, and broadly middle class, hardcore punks gathered at hardcore venues throughout the suburban sprawl for performances by such bands as the Circle Jerks, the Adolescents, and the Minutemen.

Part of this suburban shift relates to the particular geography and demographics of Southern California, where suburbia was no longer suburbia. Beginning in the 1960s, suburban areas of Southern California (and the rest of the country) underwent changes that would lead, by the 1980s, to the characterization of many such areas as a new social formation: exurbia, edge cities, or postsuburbia. The areas outlying Los Angeles were no longer simply bedroom communities servicing the center city, but full-scale, contained regions. In the postwar era alone, Orange County (south of L.A.) went from rural to suburban to postsuburban. The new types of localities contained industry (increasingly information-technology oriented), office parks, services, and shopping centers, as well as housing tracts. For bored teenagers, though, this new type of psychogeography represented the worst combination of suburban exile with posturban desolation.

At the same time as the new social formation of postsuburbia was developing, the lives of young people were changing dramatically in the aftermath of the sixties and the aging of the baby boomers. Adolescents coming of age in the 1970s faced a new set of social, political, and economic expectations and opportunities. Hardcore punk reflected as well the changes in the experiences of young people and the discourse of "youth culture" in the aftermath of the 1960s. Whereas in the fifties and sixties, young people could identify themselves as part of a generational cohort—either in rebellion against or enmeshed in the "mass culture" of American society—by the mid-1970s young people saw themselves only as individuals, with little attachment to any larger group or society. Hardcore punk reflected this individualism, creating a complex and contradictory political stance. Hardcore punks did not go to the city to enact their alienation in the traditional manner of bohemians, avant-gardists, and even earlier punk rockers. They stayed home, reviling yet—importantly— attempting to transform their postsuburban environment in the process. Punks tried to affect their environment by fashioning a violent, individualist, antipolitical politics of refusal.

The ideologies of youth culture and mass culture failed to unify young people in the seventies and eighties, nor did the institutions of family, school, work, and consumption. Hardcore punks cohered, instead, around their localized, but interconnected, scenes, coming together over a shared feeling produced by a particular musical form.[3] At the same time, however, the scenes were sites for contestation over values, aesthetics, and politics. Hardcore punks in Southern California in general eschewed any attempt to expand their scenes into a universalizing "movement," focusing, instead, on continually contesting the sets of distinctions and boundaries both within the scenes and between the scenes and the outside world.

In establishing and fighting over their scenes, hardcore punks reflected, rejected, and replicated the dominant values of postsuburbia. Through the prism of the contestation over and within scenes, *Kids of the Black Hole* examines the experiences and expectations of young people in the 1970s. Further, by exploring the margins of society—a minor subculture, really, though one with continuing importance to new generations of punk rockers—the book sheds light on social, economic, and political transformations in the United States with the emergence of postsuburbia. Finally, as punk music enters its fourth decade, now accepted as part of the established history of rock 'n' roll, this book will attempt to capture and convey some of the excitement and creativity of an important and often neglected episode in that history.

KIDS of the BLACK HOLE

1 the UNHEARD MUSIC

Punk Rock Comes to Los Angeles

There was nothing going on. If you were young and looking for something to do, looking for stimulation or adventure, you might as well have been in Kansas as Los Angeles in 1977. But the young people who lived in L.A., natives and others who came from all over the country, expected something we might call culture, even in this town. "Culture" is a word notoriously hard to define, but what better word would you choose? Young people came to L.A. because it seemed like a place where they could do something, *be* something, create themselves anew amid a whirl of ideas, images, myths, and other culture seekers, other culture creators. Maybe it was the end of the line; maybe it was the beginning of the fulfillment of dreams. They came for the same reason people had been coming since Nathanael West and Budd Schulberg described the place in the 1930s and even before: because there was still, in the 1970s, nowhere else to go. They were like the people who had come during the Depression, leaving nothing behind, coming to find something, or so they thought, but finding nothing there. But this time they did not come believing in the Hollywood dream-factory dream. Whether they came to chase their ambitions or to end their worlds, they arrived in a twisted Technicolor noir world, and when they searched their memories for images or ideas to explain what they saw, Raymond Chandler made some sense, but so did the Monkees. But none of it made enough sense. There was nothing going on.

And the younger among them were foolish enough to think that something *should* be going on.

"You really don't care what you do when you get there. You figure you're gonna get a job and meet some interesting people, and you'll get involved with artists and poets and things, and maybe you'll get famous being an artist, or make a living at it," remembered Exene Cervenka, founding member of the punk band X.[1] Her future husband and bandmate recalled: "I got to Los Angeles on Halloween of 1976. On New Year's Eve of '76, I thought, well, I think I'll go down and see this pretty girl I know, Exene. I was walking down the street in Venice and got jumped. I beat the crap out of these two kids, but not before they had pulled their belts off and whanged me over the head about thirty times. So I walked into this bar, and there were all these old people with party hats on, really loaded. The blood was running down my face, and I walked into the bathroom and washed my face off. Then I went to this other party and saw this whore woman, and she climbed up a pine tree and started humping one of the stumps. It was just hideous, gruesome. And I just thought . . . this is California."[2] Or, at least, this was the California of Charles Bukowski or Joan Didion, the seamy, desiccated underside of the sunshine and swimming pool dream.

Los Angeles did have its cultural traditions, including the thriving R&B scenes of the forties and fifties and the Sunset Boulevard psychedelic sound of the sixties. But by the mid-1970s nothing was left that anyone could see from street level. Hollywood existed only in the imagination, or behind the closed doors of the culture factories and in dissociated and surreal images dotted throughout the landscape. You might catch a glimpse of the set for *Hello, Dolly!* or countless westerns if you peeked over the walls at Twentieth Century Fox or Paramount. You might drive by the Beverly Hillbillies' mansion in Bel Air or stately Wayne Manor in Hancock Park, but all they revealed was how much bigger things looked on television.

Music? You want music? Forget the radio, unless you are willing to settle for the laid-back sounds of posthippie, studio-professional cool. In the clubs were folkies like Batdorf & Rodney and Joni Mitchell. On the charts the Eagles, Jackson Browne, and Linda Ronstadt blended folk, country, and the easy-listening rock 'n' roll of faceless, session musicians. This is what the sixties rebellion had produced? Sure, Walter Becker and

Donald Fagen of Steely Dan are *geniuses*, but, jeez, I wanna rock! I don't need my music with footnotes, man.

Or, at least, that is how a disconnected minority of young people in the L.A. area—and across the country—was beginning to feel by the mid-seventies.

I was not one of them, at least not initially. I was barely a teenager at the time, living in a fairly affluent neighborhood near Hollywood. I ate Wonder Bread, watched *The Brady Bunch*, and listened to rock radio. Raised on the Allman Brothers, Rolling Stones, Jethro Tull (all thanks to an older brother), I spent a lot of time listening to rock. One of my earliest memories is of rocking on my hands and knees to the Beatles on 45-rpm singles. The first album I bought with my own money was the Who's *Tommy*. At my first concert, at age twelve, by the encore I was jumping up and down on my chair—out of my mind—as Lynyrd Skynyrd played "Free Bird."

In December of 1977, my friend Rob and I went to see the Ramones at the Whisky a Go-Go on the Sunset Strip. I was only fifteen, so Rob drove. I don't recall whose idea it was—maybe mine, because I would prove to be the one who was most interested in new music. We had been hearing about punk, occasionally passing on the dismissive comments we heard about it, but we hadn't heard the music itself, as far as I can remember. And we weren't the type to go to clubs, where you had to go to hear punk music. We were rockers. A few months before, Rob and I saw Led Zeppelin at the L.A. Forum, a sporting arena that could seat 20,000-plus. From my seat in the third-to-last row, I peered down at the band, tiny dots on a far-off stage barely visible through the haze of pot. I watched stoned-out fans tumble down the stairs while Jimmy Page and John Bonham performed endless guitar and drum solos. I was bored.

We stepped into the Whisky and found ourselves standing right in front, leaning on the stage. I couldn't believe it was possible to get so close. Then the Ramones hit the stage. 1-2-3-4, and the sound just exploded against my face as Johnny Ramone thwacked his guitar not five feet from my head. I turned to the right and saw the crowd burst into a frenzy of pogo dancing—up and down, up and down, pinging upright into each other and then going down in a heap, writhing on the floor until they picked each other up and pogoed and pogoed and pogoed some more. The girls screamed for Dee Dee Ramone; the crowd flicked cigarette butts onto the stage—apparently the local punk gesture, a replacement for the spitting that punks did in England. They all seemed to be having a lot of fun, but I wasn't sure what to make of them.

I wasn't sure what to make of the whole scene. I liked the Ramones, but I spent most of the show eyeing the smoldering cigarette butts on the stage, gauging how close they were to wires and amps. Rob and I agreed afterward that we really liked the opening band, Moon Martin, because they had three guitarists—now, *that* was rock 'n' roll I could understand. I knew something was going on here, but I didn't quite know what it was. And I didn't think that it was for me. These people were from a different world, or so I thought. Over the next couple of years, I occasionally listened to punk music. I was the one among my friends who bought albums by Elvis Costello, Nick Lowe, the Clash, the Ramones, and the Sex Pistols. My best buddies would occasionally humor me by allowing me to play a song or two on the record player while we were hanging out. But then it was back to Yes, Pink Floyd, Bad Company, Foreigner, et al. I couldn't agree yet with punks that Zeppelin was "dinosaur rock," but I did, tentatively, explore their music.

I bought my first records by local punk bands—the Dickies' ten-inch EP; the compilation album *Tooth and Nail;* albums by the Germs and the Flesh Eaters—at the Licorice Pizza record store on Sunset. And, most importantly, I bought every issue of the local punk magazine *Slash* that I could find, along with occasional copies of national rock mags like *Trouser Press, Creem,* and *Circus* at Music Plus on Cahuenga Boulevard. *Slash* messed with my mind. I read every word, from cover to cover, because I had no frames of reference for distinguishing between different types of content. Who *were* these old blues artists they were writing about? What was this thing called reggae? All these incredibly strange-looking people, anarchic graphics, and prose the likes of which no teacher had ever exposed me to.

One photograph sticks in my mind to this day. It showed the top of a head, shaved into a reverse Mohawk, with hair on the sides and a buzz line down the middle. Lying on the shaved part was a slab of liver. What the fuck was *that*? Beyond the music, I was being introduced to an attitude, an aesthetic sense, and a subculture, although I didn't know it at the time.

In the spring of '79 my friend Steve pulled me toward the scene. His older friend Paul had recently taken him to see X and the Dead Kennedys. We saw a few shows at the Whisky—the Go Gos, the Plugz (the coolest), and Black Randy and the Metrosquad doing the Village People's "Macho Man" (with Randy looking like an accountant at the start of the set, then stripping to his bikini briefs and holster for the encore). On St. Patrick's Day, Steve and I drove to Encino to pick up Paul. He walked out of his family's suburban bungalow dressed head to toe in leather, a pint of Bacardi 151 in his pocket—now, *that* was punk rock! I was in my jeans and flannel shirt. We drove to downtown L.A., across from MacArthur Park, to see a punk rock show at the Elks Lodge.

But you will have to read the rest of the book to find out what happened there. I tell my story not to establish my bona fides but to get back to how I missed it. How could I miss it? Not until a couple of years later, in college and in the Bay Area, did I start to really absorb what was going on. And then I *didn't* miss it. I saw amazing bands doing amazing things time and time again. Flipper, Dead Kennedys, Toiling Midgets, Crucifix, Fang, and all the bands that came through. Mabuhay Gardens, 10th St. Hall, the Elite Club, On Broadway, IBeam, and Sound of Music. I saw plenty of lousy, amateurish bands, too, but often enjoyed them just as much.

But why did I miss it earlier? Well, I was young and I couldn't drive. But also I didn't think it was *mine*. These people were older, cooler, *realer* than me. I wasn't like them, and could never be. They came from somewhere else.

Of course, I was wrong. They came from places just like mine, and from the vast range of the broad middle class of postsuburban Southern California.

"Blank Generation"

While Detroit and Cleveland merit recognition for their proto-punk scenes with bands like the Stooges, the MC5, Electric Eels, and Rocket from the Tombs, and while other bands such as the Modern Lovers and Velvet Underground deserve their status as forefathers of punk, it was in 1974 in New York, at a bar on the Bowery called CBGB, that punk came into existence as a musical form at the center of a social scene.[3] In the context of the mellow, countrified sounds of the Eagles and the highly textured, expansively produced sounds of disco and rock—the music that dominated the charts, clubs, and radio playlists—bands like the Ramones sounded revolutionary. And with song titles like "Beat on the Brat," "Gimme Shock Treatment," and "Blitzkrieg Bop," the Ramones created a cartoonish thug persona in direct defiance of the reigning lyrical conventions of love and fantasy. While there was a fairly wide range of noises emanating from CBGB on the Bowery—from the avant-garde to subcultural populist—the New York bands shared an urban sensibility, an urbanism defined by rust, graffiti, and fiscal bankruptcy. Situated in New York, the punk scene garnered its share of attention and commentary, but the music did not make a dent in the pop music charts.

When the Ramones toured England in 1976, they received the attention they lacked in the United States, and they left in their wake a slew of new bands throughout London (and then in the northern industrial cities of England): the Sex Pistols, created and managed by Malcolm McLaren, who previously managed the proto-punk band the New York Dolls and then owned the boutique Sex on Kings Road; the Clash, former pub-rockers turned punks; The Damned, Slaughter and the Dogs, the Subway Sect, Siouxsie and the Banshees, the Adverts, X-Ray Spex, the Buzzcocks, and more. But the impact of the Ramones was felt far beyond the world of rock 'n' roll.

Musically, many British punk bands embraced the stripped-down-to-the-basics power chords and minimalist beat of the punk rock of the Ramones. In this way, British punk was, first of all, a return of rock 'n' roll to its roots—not just the roots in the bayous, swamps, and hill country of the American South, but the roots in the basement or garage. Punk rock was three or four guys and gals pounding away on their electrified instruments with a minimum of skill and a maximum of enthusiasm. Punk rock was to be played live, with little technological and professional intervention, not in the studio to be manipulated by technicians. Anyone could do it.

As a musical form, punk linked a return to musical roots with a rejection of the self-importance of the overblown production styles and ideologies of the established rock stars of the sixties. When, in the mid-sixties, the Beatles, the Beach Boys, Bob Dylan, and the Grateful Dead competed for musical seriousness, rock 'n' roll was rechristened as Rock, a sound and a movement with artistic and social importance. Punks discarded the claims that rock was art and the basis of a youth movement. As the punk journalists Julie Burchill and Tony Parsons argued in their 1978 obituary of rock 'n' roll, "Rock had bartered its purity and vulgarity for rais-

The Ramones, America's archetypal punk band, at the Whisky a Go-Go, February 1977.

© Jenny Lens Punk Archive/Cache Agency.

ing of consciousness and respectability."[4] Punks subverted the optimism espoused by both the marketers and the rockers of the sixties generation. As New York's Richard Hell and the Voidoids sang, "I belong to the blank generation / I can take it or leave it each time." The "blank generation" was as yet undefined, as in "fill in the blank." Indeed, the "blank generation" was indefinable: "blank" meant "I don't care," "No Feelings," "No Values," "I Wanna Be Sedated," as the punk song titles put it, not a generation at all, but an aggregation of individuals saying no to everything. "Please Kill Me" announced Richard Hell's T-shirt, and Johnny Rotten scrawled "I hate" above the Pink Floyd logo on his T-shirt.

The politics of punk rock was more complex than a simple negation. It was the apotheosis of the postwar "revolt through style." Punk combined the music and fashion of postwar Britain, then deconstructed and recombined them in a postmodern "bricolage," a random assemblage of the best and detritus of society, thereby calling attention to the very constructedness of society and society's truths. As numerous critics have shown, punk drew on the ideology of the Situationists of the 1960s to critique the social order. Punk attempted "a negation of all social facts," in pursuit of a "detournement" to overturn the accepted meanings of the artifacts of the dominant ideology. Unlike in New York, where punk made little impact on, say, the bicentennial celebration of 1976, London punks explicitly politicized their social situation, especially the events designed to mark the Queen's Silver Jubilee in 1977, a celebration that seemed to punks a mockery in a period of decline.[5]

More and more people throughout the world adopted punk as their own and shaped its sound, style, and ideology to their own purposes. In the United States, punk remained a marginal music and a small subculture throughout the seventies and eighties—failing to reach mainstream ears until Nirvana's 1991 album *Nevermind*—but it expressed a variety of dissatisfactions that young people felt. When punk arrived in Los Angeles in the late seventies, some people were ready to embrace its musical form and its expression of their sense of the world. For those whose eyes and ears were open, who were waiting for something to happen in a world where nothing was happening, punk rock offered an alternative, as music, as vision, as culture. From 1977 through the 1980s, punk rock spoke to more and more young people throughout Southern California, embodying their experiences, shaping their identities. They craved a personal connection to their music and a music that could express their sense of the world.

Although L.A. punk descended from New York and London punk, the local scene did not simply materialize. There were a number of local pioneers and forerunners who paved the way. Among them were several people who had already been trying to make a go of it musically outside the set channels of the music biz.

Rodney Bingenheimer was especially influential. After stints as a stand-in for Davy Jones of the Monkees and as a West Coast promoter for David Bowie, he opened Rodney's English Disco on Sunset Boulevard in 1972, trying to bring the latest trend on the British charts—glam rock, called glitter in L.A.—to the locals. Celebs like charter member Bowie, Keith Moon, the members of Led Zeppelin, Linda Blair, and Shaun Cassidy

Greg Shaw, Vickie (of Venus and the Razor Blades), and Rodney Bingenheimer in 1977.
© Jenny Lens Punk Archive/Cache Agency.

hung out in the VIP room, while "glitter kids" from the other side of the Hollywood Hills in the San Fernando Valley or down the coast as far as San Pedro scurried around the dance floor.[6] These kids had never experienced the sixties, didn't give a shit about them. Dressed to the nines in their tightest, shiniest, wildest finery, they were just old enough to catch a ride in from the Valley, convince someone to buy them a six-pack at the liquor store, get drunk, then pop some Quaaludes. These kids headed out to Rodney's to prance and dance. The older ones, holding on as the peace and love of the sixties slid into the cocaine, hot tubs, and Erhard Seminars Training (est) of the seventies, came too.

The gathering at Rodney's was small enough that a sense of community could develop, especially between the performers and fans. David Bowie, for example, was an enormous rock star who sold out a weeklong series of shows at the Universal Amphitheatre with an elaborate and expensive stage show, but he liked to go to Rodney's to spin discs .[7] Yet the small "scene," such as it existed, of rock stars and fans hanging out together did not affect the bloated rock world with its egotistical stars, the world that arose after the triumph of Woodstock and the tragedy of Altamont in 1969: the rock stars retreated from the VIP room at Rodney's to their suites at the Continental Hyatt House, down the road on Sunset, to ingest extraordinary amounts of coke, heroin, Quaaludes, and alcohol while abusing teenage groupies.[8]

One of Rodney's regulars was Iggy Pop, now universally acknowledged as the godfather of punk. The Detroit rocker's song titles "Search and Destroy," "Raw Power," and "I Wanna Be Your Dog" coined resonant phrases (and future titles for fanzines by California rockers and punks). Iggy combined to perfection the hard edge of rock "purity" with the theatricality of glam. He moved to L.A. in 1972 after recording the historic album *Raw Power* to be in the "glam capitol of America."[9]

Iggy usually performed onstage stripped to the waist, with tight jeans, make-up, and long hair, a paragon of freakish, gaunt androgyny. He smeared food over his body and rolled around in broken glass. Appearing on the Dinah Shore's daytime talk show in 1977, Iggy explained his violence against himself and others while on stage:

> IGGY: I was bored and angry and ugh . . . when things would get so . . . when something demanded action every day, when something kept pestering in my mind, and I couldn't do anything about it I'd just resort to simply violence.
>
> DINAH SHORE: You cut yourself with a bottle?
>
> IGGY: Yes; you see, that was because I'd done something foolish the night before and I was ashamed. I've since had treatment for that sort of thing.
>
> DINAH SHORE: Do you feel in your music you had a chance, coupled with the violence, to contribute something?
>
> IGGY: I think I've contributed something yes. I think I've helped wipe out the sixties![10]

Iggy Pop, April 1977.
© Jenny Lens Punk Archive/Cache Agency.

Though Iggy was an important musical forebear of punk, because he used rock as an outlet for rage and as an opportunity to end the sixties, by the time he moved to Los Angeles, he had lost his band and no record company would touch him. Iggy sank into a paranoid heroin addiction. Even his threat to kill himself on stage at Rodney's during his performance of "Murder of a Virgin" failed to create much of a stir among the jaded, though the resulting photos of a platinum-bleached Iggy dripping blood from the gashes on his chest ultimately cemented his legend.

Rodney's closed in 1975. When his dj moved to the Sugar Shack, a new all-ages club just over the hill in North Hollywood, to spin disco records, it seemed that glitter did not lead to a renaissance of live rock 'n' roll, but to disco.

In the summer of 1975, the Runaways played their first gig in the living room of a home in Torrance owned by the parents of Phast Phreddie Patterson, a cofounder of *Back Door Man*, a fanzine for hardcore rock 'n' roll. (The magazine covered the good music ignored by the record industry and the mainstream music press, from the bluesman Howlin' Wolf to Cleveland avant-gardists Pere Ubu.) A band of teenage girls led by Joan Jett, the Runaways were more than a gimmick. Behind the jailbait, cherrybomb façade, they played real rock 'n' roll, not all of it inspired, but enough of it damn near perfect. Real, live rock 'n' roll, with some nod toward creativity, was still an all-too-rare commodity in a town where rock clubs booked only cover bands. The Runaways were managed by producer and promoter Kim Fowley, a scenester holdover from the sixties and would-be Svengali, purveying rock'n'roll to the masses as he scrambled to book live rock shows around town.

A smattering of other rockers tried to break through the torpor, forming real bands and booking their own shows, indeed renting spaces to play in. A couple of Runaway groupies and acid freaks from University High, Jan Paul Beahm and George Ruthenberg, formed a fake band called "Sophistifuck and The Revlon Spam Queens," but couldn't afford to print up band T-shirts with that many letters. A handful of bands billing themselves collectively as Radio Free Hollywood—the Pop!, the Dogs, Max Laser and the Motels—performed wherever and whenever they could.

Without a live venue, Rodney took to the airwaves, launching his own radio show on August 16, 1976, by blasting the Ramones out of the Pasadena Hilton Hotel on AM and FM on KROQ. He tapped into a desire the major record companies did not even know existed, even when it was expressed right in their own backyard (or parking lot, as the Capitol Records swap meet on Vine Street, just off Hollywood Boulevard, was the place to be on Saturday nights if you were a devotee, collector, freak, cognoscente, or seeker). KROQ also produced shows featuring local bands like Venus and the Razorblades (another Kim Fowley creation) and the Quick, who drew three thousand people for a performance at the Bel-Air Sands Hotel—an extraordinary turnout for a band with no airplay or record contract. Peter Case and the Nerves opened the Hollywood Punk Palace, holding their first show in the basement of the Columbia Pictures lot with pioneering local glamster Zolar-X. Their second show early in 1977 at the SIR Studios soundstage, was called the Punk Rock Invasion and featured the Weirdos, Dils, Zippers, and a New York band called Short Ice. Searching high and low for places to play, Case finally rented the Orpheum across from the Whisky a Go-Go, the famed Sunset Strip club where bands like Love and the Doors had performed in the sixties, but whose owner refused to book punk.

Greg Shaw was another pioneer who, as he had since the mid-sixties, tirelessly promoted through his fanzines and record productions whatever rock 'n' roll that sounded to him like *real* rock 'n' roll. His Bomp Records store in North Hollywood was one of the few places rockers might come in contact with New York and British punk and other obscure and dispersed signs of life in rock 'n' roll. Others toiled in equally dismal environs, looking for ways to express themselves and organize their existences through art schools, poetry workshops, gay performance, and, wherever possible, rock 'n' roll. As videographer Black Randy remembered of his return from New York to L.A. in 1974, "Like everybody else in the mid-'70s, I was wishing that something would happen that would shake us free of the legacy of the hippies, and that there would be something new and there would be excitement again instead of disillusionment and total apathy."[11] Scattered throughout the southland were kids and young adults waiting for something to happen. "I had a hankering it was coming," Cliff Roman of the Weirdos remembers. "I just knew. We saw the Ramones and we had their album and we were reading about The Clash and the Sex Pistols, Generation X and The Damned, but never heard them. Rodney would be talking about them, even before he played their records and stuff."[12]

Left to right: (partly out of frame) Pleasant Gehman, Weirdo Dave Trout, Lorna Doom, Jan Paul Beahm, and (seated) Pat Smear, in the Bomp! Records Store on April 16, 1977, the day of The Damned's appearance.

© Jenny Lens Punk Archive/Cache Agency.

The forces that would unify the Los Angeles punk scene coalesced on April 16, 1977, when The Damned—the first English punk band to appear on vinyl—made an appearance at the Bomp Records store on Laurel Canyon. Rodney Bingenheimer was there. So was KK Barrett, leader of an artsy techno-sonic ensemble transplanted from Seattle called the Screamers. The Uni High glitter boys Jan Paul Beahm and George Ruthenberg (rechristened with the punk monikers Bobby Pyn and Pat Smear) met members of the Weirdos, Cal Arts students who had booked the Orpheum for their first appearance in Hollywood proper. To play before them, the Weirdos had signed on the Zeros, a group of Mexican American kids from San Diego, and they needed another band even worse than their own to open the show. They offered the spot to Pyn and Smear's band, now called the Germs—a name that *could* fit on a T-shirt.[13]

The Germs prepared for the show not by rehearsing (as they had yet to actually practice any songs) but by drinking Andre Cold Duck pink champagne and eating Quaaludes. When the show began, the band wrapped Bobby in licorice and smeared him with peanut butter as he paced the stage. Pat Smear "wrenched out bone-crunching noise" on his guitar. Lorna Doom (Terry Ryan—whom Pat and Bobby had met while trying to get an autograph from Queen's lead singer, Freddie Mercury) occasionally slapped at the bass while swigging champagne. Very little music was made, but noise and spectacle were. Allegedly the police were summoned, the Germs were kicked offstage, and a legend was launched. In their three and a half years as a band, the Germs would play barely a gig without the intervention of the police, usually at the behest of a terrified club owner.[14] But on this night the Zeros and Weirdos followed and The Damned's Captain Sensible jumped up on stage to jam and to consecrate L.A. punk. *Time* snapped a backstage photo of the Weirdos for an upcoming punk spread, in which the magazine admitted that "despite some of the revolting accoutrements, there is real musical value in much of punk rock."[15] Finally there was proof positive that punk existed in the land of angels.

Or, at the very least, a founding myth was framed, as this show became a catalyst for the L.A. punk scene. "The first punk show I saw was the Zeros and the Germs and the Weirdos," recalled Alice Armendariz, who would soon become Alice Bag, lead singer of the Bags. "I was just sold. Here were people my own age doing something different and exciting

Kim Fowley (right) with unidentified woman outside Bomp! Records store in North Hollywood, April 16, 1977.
© Jenny Lens Punk Archive/Cache Agency.

and new. The Germs had peanut butter up onstage and they smeared it all over each other. They didn't really play. I don't remember it being musical as much as performance."[16] Two nights later as The Damned played, their manager ran onstage yelling, "You fat Americans in your Cadillacs disgust me!" and, as one new punk described the scene, "Rat Scabies had baby powder on his drum set so there was a big cloud around him and Captain Sensible was always pulling down his pants or taking a piss onstage. That was all the norm."[17]

Alice Bag, lead singer of the Bags, at Elks Lodge benefit, February 24, 1978.
© Jenny Lens Punk Archive/ Cache Agency.

As L.A. punk Craig Lee recounted in the first insider chronicle of the scene, *Hardcore California*, published in 1983, when The Damned arrived in April 1977 and "charged through the sloppy, intense, shambles of a set at the Starwood, the L.A. kids immediately picked up on the energy and theatricality of the band. It was making them FEEL SOMETHING. By the end of The Damned set, people looked around, some with a shock of recognition on their faces. Bonds were forming. The poseurs were being separated from the possessed."[18] Chip Kinman of the Dils said, "After those shows you knew you had to make a choice. You had to either fish or cut bait. That's when you got the first group of punks."[19] This was the moment when, according to Lee, "a definite punk core was forming" in Los Angeles, a core that distinguished L.A. punk as something cohesive and distinctive. The people were there, and then came the ideology, as it were. As Lee put it, "L.A punks were instigating fashion anarchy and musical chaos as a way of striking back at the complacent, dull scene they had suffered for the last decade."[20]

The L.A. punk movement would be an artistic rebellion, a revival of rock 'n' roll rebellion, and a place for various avant-gardists, bohemians, and weirdos to all come together—a centralizing force for mobile youth in a town with no physical center.

L.A. punk music spoke to the city of L.A, to its vastness, its amorphousness, its racism and segregation, its inhumanity. L.A. punk spoke as well to London and New York punk, adopting their styles, but twisting and turning them, building a tradition in collegiality and camaraderie. L.A. punk also had a dialogue with San Francisco punk, which was contemporaneously creating its own analogous, uniquely S.F.-flavored punk. It spoke to the rock 'n' roll institutions: the local music stranglehold over radio and studios, the laid back Cali style, the burgeoning disco-ification, the lack of local clubs to play live, and rock traditions, especially the local one, drawing upon the musical history of, for example, the Whisky a Go-Go. In this vein, it spoke dramatically to the ghost of Jim Morrison, lead singer of the Doors, who no doubt spoke back, so that probably at least half the male singers of punk bands considered themselves poets and shamans. And wider than this, it responded to the whole arts environment of the L.A. area, as this poetic infusion into L.A. punk came not only through the Doors influence, but also from the influence of the Venice Beach cafe poetry scene and the gay performance art scene, which provided inspiration for much of the aesthetic of L.A. punk.

Punk responded thus to the wider cultural influences of L.A.: the freeways, the architecture, the driving, the driving, the driving, passing through segregated neighborhoods on the way to work, to a club, to a place to catch a view while getting high. And, of course, L.A. punk responded to Hollywood, both as a real world locale and through the refracted prism of television, where the houses seen on television weekly, the mansions in Hancock Park and Bel Air, the palm trees of Beverly Hills, the strips of the barrios . . . all this came to life twice. And L.A. punk responded to Hollywood with irony.

The first Los Angeles punks combined and adapted much of the style, ideology, and sound of both New York and London punk to create their own distinctive subcultural scene. As a musical, artistic, bohemian expression in New York, punk opposed the stagnation of mainstream rock 'n' roll. In England, punk became an important social phenomenon because it spoke to working-class anger and anomie at a specific moment in British history: punk seemed to signify on an everyday level the larger political significance of the breakdown of both the postwar welfare state and the empire as a whole. In Los Angeles, there were some people looking for something exciting to do and there were some people listening for some new rock 'n' roll. Drawn to punk rock in Los Angeles because punk, imported from New York and London, seemed to fulfill both needs, they established a "scene," redesigning punk to fit their particular local situation. And the scene became a scene when it established who was in and who was out. When The Damned came to town and the Weirdos and Germs played in Hollywood in the spring of 1977, the moment to jump in had arrived.

"So This is War, Eh?"

Inspired by the happenings in London, Steve Samiof and Melanie Nissen, members of the small underground art scene, produced a punk magazine called *Slash* even before The Damned arrived. They prevailed upon Claude Bessy, a French dishwasher and the editor of the reggae-inspired fanzine *Angelino Dread,* to edit it. "I was just typing my little head off," Bessy said of *Angelino Dread,* "and Xeroxing and sending it to friends.

Claude Bessy (Kickboy Face), the editor of *Slash*.
© Jenny Lens Punk Archive/ Cache Agency.

(Opposite) The January 1978 issue of *Slash*.
© Jenny Lens Punk Archive/ Cache Agency.

But I'm talking original fanzine. I was paying for the Xerox, paying for the mailing. And then somebody contacted me and said, 'I've just read this newsletter you're putting out, and I like your attitude,' which was really nasty. And he said, 'I'm starting a magazine about punk rock.' And I thought, 'What the fuck is punk rock?'" [21]

Though Bessy had never heard punk music before, when Samiof put a Damned record on the record player, Bessy got it right away. He assumed the editorship of *Slash* with his girlfriend Philomena Winstanley, an Englishwoman who came to L.A. in 1974 to visit and had never left after Claude convinced her to spend her return fare on tequila. Assuming the pseudonym Kickboy Face, Bessy became "the leading voice of *Slash*'s literary reign of terror." [22]

Bessy titled his very first editorial, dated "Mayday 1977," "So This is War, Eh?" *Slash*, he wrote, "was born out of curiosity and out of hope. Curiosity regarding what looks like a possible rebirth of true rebel music, hope in its eventual victory over the bland products professional pop stars have been feeding us. May the punks set this rat-infested industry on fire." In its pursuit of "true rebel music," *Slash* articulated a hatred of the established music business. Anchoring its definition of punk in a "war" against

VOLUME 1 NUMBER 7   JANUARY 1978   FIFTY CENTS

the record industry, it denounced the music that the business had produced in the 1970s, above all progressive rock, with its "concept albums,"
its "cosmic discoveries," and its "pseudo-philosophical inanities"; and "the
dreadful dripping sounds of disco," with its emphasis on technological
fetishism and professional artisanship over performance and emotion.
The "punk revolution" embraced the "dirty primitive music that has little
to do with the stuff music stations have been pouring in our ears for what
seems to be an eternity."[23]

Slash disdained not only the corporate music industry, but also the
sixties counterculture from which had emerged the rock commodity.
If the sixties provided a model for social protest, for punks the decade
was as much an emblem of the overindulgence of the L.A., or American,
culture of narcissism that the historian Christopher Lasch identified at
the time.[24] Disco was thus a direct outgrowth of sixties hedonism.[25] Yet
L.A. punks mostly rebelled against the contemporary rock 'n' roll world,
which was dominated by progressive rock. As the Weirdos sang in "Destroy All Music": "Sold my records and my stereo / Ripped up my tickets
to see E.L.O.!" E.L.O. (Electric Light Orchestra) with its grandiose fusion
of pop melodies with classical arrangements and space-age imagery, was,
of course, the worst of the "professional" progressive rock bands, partly
because, as perverse as it may seem, they saw themselves as heirs to the
Beatles.[26] Such was the damage done by the 1967 Beatles album, *Sgt. Pepper's Lonely Hearts Club Band*, which signaled rock 'n' roll was now Rock
with a capital R, something to be taken seriously as Art with a capital A.
L.A. punk explicitly rejected the technological fetishism and perfection-
ism of "art rock," which had emerged in the wake of the serious turn
taken by bands in the sixties. Punk rejected this music as well as disco
because both had destroyed rock 'n' roll aesthetically and professionally,
leaving no place to hear or produce real rock 'n' roll. The "punk revolution," then, in L.A. was first of all aimed at the music biz.

In May 1977, there was not really a punk subculture yet in L.A., but
Slash's opening editorial worked as a catalyst. "*Slash* started as a bluff,"
Bessy later recalled. "We were pretending there was an LA scene when
there was no scene whatsoever. The magazine was it. . . . Then all these
disaffected loonies started focusing on the mag and decided 'We can be
it, too.'"[27] Under Bessy's editorship, *Slash* served as a manifesto for this
punk revolution, but it also brought people together *as* punks, helping to

crystallize a "scene." As one punk remembered: "In May of '77 I saw the first issue of *Slash* and thought, 'Wow, there's a scene going on!' They kind of put it together."[28]

"The words flew out fast, furious, disconnected, a code that only those in the know could truly understand," said Craig Lee of the early *Slash*. "One felt slightly out of it if they didn't know what *Slash* was ranting about. The curious became intrigued to find those records or see those bands that *Slash* declared were the only true lights in an awfully dim world." The magazine also helped set the visual aesthetic for the scene, featuring an extraordinary drawing by Gary Panter of Tommy Gear of the Screamers. No matter that no one at *Slash* or anywhere else had ever *heard* the Screamers yet: "If *Slash* said so, then the Screamers were IT!"[29] "Resolutely committed to the anger and fury of Punk . . . [with] an almost Biblical fire-and-brimstone righteousness,"[30] *Slash* provided the signature L.A. punk voice.

Screamers logo.
Courtesy of Gary Panter.

In the summer of 1977 Brendan Mullen opened the Masque, giving budding punks a place to gather and make the music that provided the core of the developing punk scene. Mullen described himself as a "young, white, under-educated, unemployed, Scottish-Irish hippie illegal immigrant—not terrifically talented or gifted in any specific way and, as is the curse of the under-achiever with too much time . . . bored, bored, desperately BORED." Wandering the streets of Hollywood, he discovered behind the Pussycat Theater the Hollywood Center Building, an art deco office building built by Cecil B. DeMille in 1926. It had a large basement that "consisted of a labyrinth of corridors and rooms of different shapes and sizes." "The legend turned in his grave as anti-beauty moved into his basement to trash glamour and everything the old Hollywood was founded upon."[31]

On July 1, Mullen leased the basement and began to clear out the debris that had been left fifteen years earlier by the last tenant. He took out an ad announcing "radically cheap rehearsal facilities." The newly installed pay phone rung off the hook with calls from musicians of every type from all over the L.A. area.[32] That week, Mullen was approached by a member of the Skulls who wanted a place to play for some people from a magazine

Brendan Mullen in 1978.
© Jenny Lens Punk Archive/Cache Agency.

called *Slash*. "And so," Mullen remembered, "the Skulls thrashed in darkness for five or ten people from *Slash* magazine including one noticeably-inebriated Frenchman, a gnarly Boho dishwasher from Venice Beach, and his sidekick, a swarthy Jewish-Italian salesman/huckster type, also from Venice, who chain-smoked unfiltered Camels and peppered wise-ass remarks with bad puns. . . . The frog pontificated relentlessly about 'pink' and the 'pink movement' in London. It took a while before it dawned on me that 'pink' was the Gallic enunciation of the word PUNK."[33] The frog was, of course, Claude Bessy, and his sidekick was Steve Samiof.

Another call came from a newly arrived "long-haired gnarler," according to Mullen, from Michigan named Kid Spike. He had put together a punk band named the Controllers, and they were hoping to perform at the Orpheum Theater, where the Germs and Weirdos had played just a few months earlier. Mullen offered them a show at his new space. "On an impulse I asked the Controllers what they thought if I had a stage built and we invited some people over for a no-big-deal BYOB type party that weekend—would they consider playing? The band looked at each other as if I'd just told them they'd won the lottery."[34]

That weekend, the Controllers played at the first official party/show in front of about twenty people at the newly named Masque. Among the crowd were members of the Skulls, Screamers, the Weirdos, and the Bags. The Masque hosted its second show the following weekend, experiencing the first of many run-ins with the forces of local law enforcement. As the Bags, the Controllers, the Skulls, and the Eyes played for about forty people (close to half of whom were in the four bands), outside "a bunch of drunken punks lay down all over the sidewalk . . . thus attracting the attention of the LAPD who demanded to see a permit. One of the kids began issuing friendly greetings to the officers such as 'Pigs—fuck off and die.' This diplomat went by the name of Bobby Pyn."[35] The police shut down the club and ordered Mullen to obtain a permit before reopening. Bobby Pyn, lead singer for the Germs, was thus banned from L.A.'s only punk club. Or, at least, he was banned until the Germs' manager showed Bobby's lyrics to Brendan. Words like: "I'm a lexicon devil with a battered brain / Searching for a future, the world's my aim." Words like:

> Billy Druids face is marble
> He keeps every thought in its place
> He lets the days turn tomorrow
> Someone's always walking on his grave.

Words like:

> Standing in line we're aberrations
> Defects in a defect's mirror
> And we've been here all the time real fixations
> Hidden deep in the furor—

If Bobby Pyn's persona struck Mullen as a joke and a nuisance, the lyrics spoke of a true artist, or at least a voice to be taken seriously.

On Labor Day weekend, Mullen, having obtained the required cabaret license, reopened the club with the Germs headlining. Word about the band had spread, and 150 people showed up.[36] Mullen, who had been one of those bored youth looking for something to happen, now realized what he had stumbled into: "[Bobby Pyn] blew my mind. The crowd was bouncing off the walls and he was crawling on the floor, snarling into the mike. I finally got it: It was attitude and performance. The music was secondary."[37]

The Masque became the center for a growing L.A. punk scene, with shows by the Germs, the Dickies, the Screamers, the Weirdos, Black Randy and the Metro Squad, the Alleycats, the Dils, the Zeros, the Plugz, the Deadbeats, F-Word, the Avengers (from San Francisco), and the house band of unpaid employees called Arthur J. and the Gold Cups (named for two Hollywood coffee shops frequented by gay cruisers). The Masque was, as an ad from December 1977 claimed, "A cabaret of the macabre . . . a spectacle of simulated London street desperation in the promised land filtered through a rock 'n' roll sensibility of carbonated freeway fury and terminal swimming pool despair."[38] John Denny, the Weirdos' frontman, remembered, "The smell of the Masque was just gloriously putrid. The Masque was like a funeral and a celebration all at once, the funeral being for the death of rock music as we knew it—and if you were even more committed, society as we knew it. The celebratory aspect was for the dawning of a new era."[39]

The Masque also provided L.A. punks with an identity to distinguish themselves from their more famous New York and London peers. As one punk claimed at the time, "Before the Masque everyone was intimidated by the East Coast scene. I remember a New York band playing the Whisky and putting us down as a bunch of spoiled, rich kids. . . . Well, we didn't take it. We shouted back. We're tired of people thinking everyone in L.A. is lying around Laurel Canyon, playing tennis and snorting cocaine."[40] "When we found each other at the Masque," recalled Nicole Panter, manager of the Germs, "there was a sense of cohesion."[41] That cohesion was based on a shared aesthetic—or, more accurately, a shared *approach* to aesthetics.

Calling themselves "art-damaged," punks in L.A. democratized performance art, previously an avant-garde phenomenon.[42] The politics of L.A. punk was about performance and theatricality, as, in Los Angeles, life was culture, reality was representation. Just as British punk mocked the decline of empire and protested massive unemployment, so L.A. punk celebrated the decline of Hollywood grandeur. Even the musical influences on punk were often as important for their theatrics as for their music,

Show held at the Masque, fall 1977. *(In back, with face in focus)* Robert Lopez (later El Vez), then of the Zeros.
© Jenny Lens Punk Archive/Cache Agency.

especially among those who came to punk from glam-glitter. Lee argues that the theatricality of The Damned and the other British bands attracted budding L.A. punks, setting the terms of distinction for "fashion anarchy and musical chaos." The New York punk sound and sensibility was "too cool, too pseudo-intellectual, too boring for the California set."[43] New York punks, except for the Ramones, were too enamored of Arthur Rimbaud, Paul Verlaine, and other precious nineteenth-century French poets.

L.A. bands, like the Screamers, embraced as influences "everybody from Henry Mancini and Ennio Morricone to the obvious groups like the Ramones, Velvet Underground, and the Stooges. We were trying to set ourselves apart by attitude and instrumentation. We had electric piano, drums, and synthesizer. No guitar, no bass. Our first show we had a 'klaxophone'—a keyboard made up of car horns."[44] "Punk was like when you first discover folk art as some wonderful thing," KK Barrett of the Screamers remembered. "All of a sudden you like the mistakes, the handicraft of it, the personal naiveté."[45] And, as with folk art, anyone could do it, everyone could participate. With boredom the main enemy in L.A., the revolution was aimed accordingly at it, and art would relieve the mundanity of everyday life. In the absence of any explicit political ideology, punks in L.A. established their identities as punks through the *aesthetics* of punk—the sound of the music, the style of the performance, and the emotion inspired.

The budding scene's cohesion was fortified when, early in 1978, many of the punks decided to move into the same apartment complex, located a couple of blocks away from the Masque. As *Slash* announced in the April 1978 edition of the monthly "Local Shit" column, "Rather than face the usual monthly 'too much loud music' evictions, a lot of the local contingent has been moving into the Canterbury Apts. on N. Cherokee. Now, instead of the usual 'turn it down' game, everyone's playing 'let's outdo our neighbor.' Reasonable rents, close to buses, the Masque, Hollywood Blvd.'s lovely boutiques."[46] Punks shared the Canterbury's "three stories of faded grandeur" with "black pimps and drug dealers, displaced Southeast Asians living ten to a room, Chicano families, bikers from a halfway house, in addition to various bag ladies and shopping cart men."[47] With punks renting about thirty of the apartments, the scene developed even more unity, as punks bounced from room to room fucking, drugging, and making music. "It was the first time in my life I had the feeling of belonging to something, a sense of community," Alice Bag remembered. "Here I was in the middle of a group of misfits like me—people from broken homes and runaways."[48]

Unlike mainstream rock 'n' roll, where the star and the audience existed in completely different, unconnected worlds, punk rockers were all part of a community of "stars." The Canterbury fostered the punk spirit of community and the breakdown of barriers between performer and fan. "The Masque started attracting a faithful audience and people in bands," Geza X recalled. "They were your next-door neighbors and your idols at the same time so all the barriers between star and the audience were completely shattered. It was the same thing at the Canterbury: You'd be living next door to someone in a band you absolutely idolized—and this was someone you ate dinner with. So like your best friend was also your biggest hero."[49] But this cohesion only went so far. Punk identities were framed as much by what punk was not, or what punk was against. The democratization of art coexisted with elitism, cohesion with exclusion. Like other subcultures—and like punk subcultures before them—L.A. punks had a keen sense of the distinction between insiders and outsiders.

"Subcultural ideologies are a means by which youth imagine their own and other social groups, assert their distinctive character and affirm that they are not anonymous members of an undifferentiated mass," says sociologist Sarah Thornton. And such attempts at differentiation "are never just assertions of equal difference; they usually entail some claim to authority and presume the inferiority of others."[50] L.A. punks as a group tried to set themselves apart and establish what Thornton calls "subcultural capital" by asserting their unified opposition to mainstream music and their disdain for the masses, who settled for whatever the music business shoved into their ears. Once the local punk scene was established, however, it always faced internal problems with definitions and hierarchies.

Contestation may be the only thing that unites all punk across space and time, especially contestation over what is punk, and by late 1977, barely months into a recognizable L.A. scene, the definition of a "real punk" was being fiercely contested. "At this point the Punk scene had become very in-bred and cliquish," Craig Lee wrote a few years later. "There was a lot of talk about who was a 'poseur' and who wasn't. Commitment and sincerity were essential, and one had to have punk credibility to join the clan."[51] What Lee termed "self-destructive protectiveness" resulted in a fruitless attempt to maintain control over the scene, the meaning of punk, and the sound of the music. But the exclusiveness of what he called the "Hollywood 50"—the small, in-group of punks who frequented the Masque—contained several contradictions.

If "style dictated commitment," as Lee argued, then all it took was style to demonstrate commitment. Further, part of what L.A. punk attempted to do was to "break through the limited music scene barriers," by trying to be something other than hip, which was all the typical rocker wanted to be. To be punk you had to adopt the style, but you had to commit to more than style as well. But those who found community and cohesion in the punk scene also wanted to exclude others. "Gangs"—more like cliques—of girls and young women, with names like the Piranhas and the Plungers, squared off against one another in the halls of the Canterbury and the Masque. The Hollywood 50 mocked prepunk bands like the Quick, although they shared the stages at local clubs. Still, the insiders could not control punk, which was an international phenomenon, nor could they know how tightly they should control their local scene. Barriers between the elite and the rest were permeable. The elite few, the hip insiders, inhabited the Canterbury, spent their food stamps at the corner liquor store, and frequented the Masque. But *Slash* announced this fact to "the public," to anyone who cared to pick up the magazine at a local record store. And anyone could move into the Canterbury, of course, as the "Rev" (as the punks called the Rastafarian manager) was none too picky about his tenants.

For L.A. punks the problem of distinction was exacerbated by their particular definition of punk as it was developing: punk was about commitment, but it was also about conversion. The first Hollywood punks came from all over the greater L.A. basin, traveling in to shows from over the Hollywood hills via the 101 freeway, coming from Pasadena and Whittier to the east and Venice to the west on the 10, even driving up from Fullerton, Carlsbad, and San Diego on the 405. Punks came from all over the vast, postsuburban area, but once they arrived, the rules of punk (and of youth subculture more generally) dictated that they leave their pasts and other identities behind and recreate themselves as punks. Once punks began to move into the Canterbury, punk became a full-time endeavor. Not just a style for a Saturday night on the town, like glam and disco, it was now a lifestyle to be practiced and performed all day as well as all night. Punk clothes were not to be worn only for shows, to demonstrate one's music preference, but all the time, to broadcast one's identity, making it impossible to be anything else but a punk.

This problem of maintaining control over the scene played out in an ironic way in Hollywood, because the problem centered on a question of authenticity in a town founded on the celebration of falsity and fantasy. The search for authenticity lies at the heart of the attempt at distinction in much of American popular culture, and the direct, unmediated communication of experience and emotion, without artifice or commercial considerations, distinguishes much of popular and unpopular music from "pop" music. As the sociologist Simon Frith put it in describing the ideology of rock music: "Rock, in contrast to pop, carries intimations of sincerity, authenticity, art—noncommercial concerns. These intimations have been muffled since rock became the record industry, but it is the possibilities, the promises, that matter."[52] Much of folk, country, jazz, rap, and rock differentiates itself from Tin Pan Alley, Broadway, or Top 40 by its emphasis on what historian Barry Shank calls "performed sincerity."[53] Punk rock was no exception. But how authenticity is structured differs according to subculture and musical category. "Music is perceived as authentic when it rings true or feels real, when it has credibility and comes across as genuine," Thornton argues, providing a revealing way of understanding the varieties of authenticities: "In an age of endless representations and global mediation, the experience of musical authenticity is perceived as a cure both for alienation (because it offers feelings of community) and dissimulation (because it extends a sense of the really 'real')." Fans value authenticity "as a balm for media fatigue and as an antidote to commercial hype."[54]

Authenticity is, then, the performance of reality and solidarity. But L.A. punk did not oppose the surrounding Tinseltown falsity simply by insisting on honesty or sincerity or authenticity, since such concepts were, people in the know knew, the most false facades that both the movies and pop music had ever designed. This is why London punk provided a greater inspiration to Los Angelenos than the New York version. Just about every New York band other than the Ramones carried an aura of sophistication, sincerity, or decadence that struck L.A. punks-to-be as faux-vérité.

Thornton also argues that authenticity has to do double work, promoting "originality and aura" while depicting what is "natural to the community or organic to the subculture." While artistic and subcultural forms of authenticity usually work together, they are not the same thing.[55] In Los Angeles, punks developed an ironic stance on authenticity—art-damaged—that allowed the tensions between the two versions to coexist, and created a bit of openness to the punk scene, a fluidity in cultural hierarchies. By early 1978, as punks were first moving into the Canterbury, the scene had solidified to some degree. There was a core group of people who called themselves punk, who found a sense of community and identity with each other. There was a cohesiveness in personnel, ideology, and artistic output, but a diversity in each as well. But the rest of the United States was beginning to hear more and more about punk, and the small core of insiders was no longer able to control the meaning of or access to it.

L.A. Punk and the End of Youth Culture

I wanna kick in the radio
I wanna bomb the record store
I said, destroy all music

"Destroy All Music," by The Weirdos (1977)

At the dawn of 1978, the English punk band the Sex Pistols embarked on a campaign to conquer America. Hoping to generate both cash and chaos, they launched a guerilla raid on the U.S. hinterlands. Thumbing their nose at both New York and Los Angeles, the Pistols ventured into the American unknown, hitting smaller burgs like Memphis and Tulsa and second-tier cities such as Atlanta, Dallas, and San Francisco. As the Pistols traveled through the South and Midwest, local, national, and British media emerged with pen, notepad, microphone, and camera to track down this phenomenon called "punk rock." In the Bay Area and Los Angeles, local television news and newspapers sought punk-looking youth for suitable quotes and visuals. L.A. punks got over their anger at being snubbed and made plans to catch the Pistols up the coast for the final show of the tour. "Everybody was anticipating the Sex Pistols' upcoming appearance in San Francisco, and it seemed like the major Punk revolution was on the verge of becoming a realistic fact instead of a small cult party," L.A. punk Craig Lee remembered. "And then the shit hit the fan."[1]

A contingent of Hollywood punks drove north to San Francisco, to join the five thousand plus who showed up at Bill Graham's Winterland Ballroom to see the Pistols. After booking his first show in 1965, a benefit for the San Francisco Mime Troupe that starred Jefferson Airplane, Graham had opened the soon-to-be legendary Fillmore Auditorium and the Fillmore East in New York, becoming the most powerful and notorious promoter on the West Coast, if not in the entire United States. Like Jann Wenner with *Rolling Stone* magazine, Graham had successfully packaged the sixties counterculture as business. A decade after the Summer of Love, his position as "rock impresario" was unchallenged. If the Sex Pistols were to going to play San Francisco, they were going to play in a "Bill Graham Presents" venue.

Under the shadow of Graham and the legacy of Haight–Ashbury, San Francisco had its own budding punk rock scene, complete with a club to play in—the Mabuhay Gardens, a Filipino restaurant in the sleazy North Beach section of town that started booking punk bands in late 1976. There were zines, such as *Search & Destroy* and *Punk Globe*, and a handful of bands like Crime, the Nuns, and the Avengers. The S.F. and L.A. scenes were cross-pollinating and mutually supportive, even though they grew from separate local traditions. The San Francisco punk scene was more beatnik-influenced, drawing on the city's political, poetic, and performance art histories. The Avengers invoked and inverted the early sixties optimism with lyrics like "We are the ones" and "Ask not what you can do for your country—what your country been doing to you?" Another S.F. punk, Jello Biafra of the Dead Kennedys (the name similarly calling attention to the postwar confluence of anxiety and optimism), ran for mayor of San Francisco and sang, with typically punk inflected irony and humor, of "Chemical Warfare" and a "Holiday in Cambodia." The brothers Chip and Tony Kinman of the Dils—who were originally from south of L.A., but had relocated to the more ideologically fitting northern locale—called for a "Class War" and yelled "I Hate the Rich." L.A. responded with Vom's "I Hate the Dils"—in typical L.A. punk ironic fashion. And Vom's Richard Meltzer, a pioneering rock critic, was enlisted to emcee the Sex Pistols show, where, festooned with a tampon box safety-pinned to his jacket, he

The Sex Pistols performing at the Winterland Ballroom,
San Francisco, January 14, 1978.
© Jenny Lens Punk Archive/Cache Agency.

was kicked offstage and out the door by Graham's forces before he could
even finish his introduction (whereupon he turned his jacket inside out
and sneaked back in).[2]

The Winterland show was a fiasco. The sound system was atrocious.
Onstage, Sid Vicious—who had been reined in by his handlers up to
that moment on the tour—was playing high on heroin, barely hitting the
strings of his bass throughout the set, his amplifier finally turned off so as
not to destroy the sound further. While drummer Paul Cook and guitarist
Steve Jones did their best to hold things together, Johnny Rotten looked
bored and annoyed, hanging onto the mike "like a man caught in a wind
tunnel."[3] Backstage, the manager of the Pistols, Malcolm McLaren, was

trying, without success, to match power-egos with heavyweight promoter Graham. And the Pistols were behaving like the rock stars they were. As they left the stage, Johnny Rotten snarled, "Ever get the feeling you've been cheated?" Had punk rock turned out to be nothing more than "the great rock 'n' roll swindle"?[4]The next day, McLaren tried to cart the band off to Brazil for a recording session and publicity opportunity with Ronnie Biggs, Britain's notorious Great Train Robber. Rotten, already at odds with McLaren, said "no thanks" (in less polite terms). In a sign of things to come, Sid Vicious, hanging out with a group of Hollywood punkettes, overdosed after the show and had to be rushed across the bay to a Marin County acupuncturist.[5] After another overdose three days later on a plane to New York, he managed to hook up with the remaining Pistols (sans Rotten) to fly to Rio.

New York punks predictably denounced the show, resentful that London punks were getting all the credit and fame for something they believed they had invented.[6] "The Winterland show was the worst Rock 'n' roll show I've ever seen," wrote Legs McNeil of the magazine *Punk* after the Pistols snubbed his request for an interview.[7] But the band's first and only album, *Never Mind the Bollocks, Here's the Sex Pistols*, had been released in the United States only two months earlier, and word of it was still spreading even as the band itself was falling apart. For those who were already part of the scene, however, any sense of ownership was slipping away. It was bad enough that punk's leaders were self-destructing, but now there were "thousands of ugly, stupid, witless suburbanites" finding their way to punk, "playing at a scene they had no commitment to."[8]

In Los Angeles, where the scene was still small and self-contained, Craig Lee had mixed feelings. He had looked forward to the tour as the moment when the "punk revolution" could move beyond its "cult status," but he was disappointed at the lack of "commitment" from those in the audience who seemed to him merely playing at punk. The Nuns and Avengers, who had opened for the Pistols at the Winterland, noted with dismay how the audience had bought into the hype surrounding the performance. Because the audience came expecting a freak show, "innocence" had been replaced with "sensationalism . . . spectacle," "punk" became the "punk circus."[9] V. Vale, who self-published *Search & Destroy*, described it as "a zombie performance, people who were already dead, reanimated for a while, going through their motions. [The Sex Pistols] were media-saturated, they'd run out of message to deliver."[10] "I mean punk went on after that, but we felt dirtied," remembered the Avengers' Penelope Houston. "We felt somehow the purity was gone."[11] Pat Ryan, bassist for the Nuns, said, "So what you had from there on in was the suburbs moving in. You had people who had a preconceived idea of what it was about, going to Winterland. People who were really not part of the scene coming in and just being voyeurs."[12]

Those who already considered themselves punks were now depressed or disturbed, but those who were just introduced were excited. Many of the people at the show were indeed merely playing at being punk, aping the media's depiction of what a punk should be. Some of them had come on a lark. But others were in the process of conversion, becoming punks just like those who had come around earlier. For neophytes, the show was the best thing they had ever seen. As one L.A. rocker wrote in his fanzine at the time, "It's real Rock 'n' roll. Forget about the media punk tag—these guys are Rockers. . . . As for what I came to see—The Pistols—they were really hot."[13] But others didn't strip things down to such pure musical terms. They embraced the show for its very punkness, swindle or no. Randy Detroit and Pleasant Gehman wrote in *Lobotomy*, "You can't look at it like it was a concert, it was an event. If you didn't go, you missed the children's crusades . . . a holy experience . . . there's no excuse for you!!! So what if you would've lost your job? . . . Big deal, your car broke down! . . . Who cares if you'd go broke? . . . So you'd live on the streets for a month or two! FUCK YOU AND YOUR PROBLEMS!!!!!"[14]

If Randy and Pleasant bubbled a little too enthusiastically for a distanced, ironic, "art-damaged" stance that had already become the L.A. norm, Kickboy Face caught the difficult position in the pages of *Slash*: "So here we were, with the pathetic choice of snubbing the snobs or being like the sheep someone obviously wanted us to be." The problem was solved, however, when "the Pistols walk on stage and they burst thru the millions of layers of hype and shit and slander that have surrounded them since the beginning of time (well, who remembers anything prior to '76?) . . . and Rotten just eases his way thru the set like an eel, playing it up, playing it down, constantly surprising the most jaded observers with his thoroughly unique approach to rock 'n' roll singing."[15] What was the threat of punk? What was the hope? As bad as the show was, it was still the closest thing to something real, not an ordinary social fact, but a disruption of the mundane. Even if the media didn't get it, and most of the audience was there for the wrong reasons, Rotten's performance was powerful enough for L.A. punks to overlook those problems.

For many of those with no prior exposure to punk, who were drawn to the Winterland by the mass media hoopla and left as punks, the show was life-changing. "I grew up thinking that everything had already happened, the Beatles, the Beach Boys, Beethoven, Bread," Gina Arnold remembers. "I grew up thinking that rock music mattered, but that everything worth hearing had already been laid down on vinyl. . . . In short, I grew up thinking I was born too late." For the kids of the seventies, who had grown up listening to the art rock and disco that followed the revolutionary music of the sixties, it didn't seem as though anything could ever again equal those earlier glorious days of rock 'n' roll. In Arnold's mind, the power of that music was such that surely "Elvis Presley crushed McCarthyism in America, the Beatles elected JFK, and the Rolling Stones were responsible for the rise and fall of Robert Kennedy. After which the Doors single-handedly ended the war in Vietnam." So her first experience with punk was a revelation: "I went to see the Sex Pistols, and from then on I knew that I'd been completely wrong. I hadn't been born late at all. It was just that everybody else had been entirely premature, doomed to incubate things for better days to come." The same performance that had ended the era of the Pistols and weakened many S.F. and L.A. punks' faith in the revolution had won over a new convert—not an artist or bohemian, not a worker on the dole, but "a tubby and insecure white suburban high schooler."[16]

Arnold did feel cheated, but not by Johnny Rotten and the Sex Pistols. As part of Richard Hell's "blank generation," she felt cheated by history, a history in which young people had seemingly harnessed mass culture to shape their own destinies and change the world, only to stop just as she was coming of age. But then she went to see the Pistols: "I went totally ballistic. A great chasm of possibility immediately yawned open, a canyon of hope that simply hadn't been there before. And I leapt into its breach, my friends. I dove on in."[17] She was ready to leave the sixties behind, insert herself into the narrative, and obliterate the whole history she had been taught. She would make history through punk rock.

Arnold's tale takes us to the center of how and *why* punk rock evolved beyond the New York and London scenes, beyond bohemia. While her knowledge of history is stunningly, even laughably, obtuse, she articulates clearly the received wisdom of many young people coming of age after the 1960s. They felt they had missed the moment when youth—within and against mass culture—had seemed at the center of American history. In order to understand punk in California, we must step back to sketch out a crucial social context—the history of youth culture, especially in its relationship to mass culture. Punk in California gave voice to a sense that young people in the 1970s were living in a specific political moment. They inhabited the end of the nexus of mass culture and youth culture that had grown over the past century or so.

Youth and Mass Culture

There has probably never been a time in American history when young people haven't worried their elders. Rejecting their parents' values and embracing radical social changes, young people have continually failed to live up to the expectations of society's leaders. Indeed, almost as soon as the first English settlers arrived in the New World, religious leaders began to fear "the rising generation" as young people rejected their elders' edicts.

In the nineteenth century, the "youth problem" in the United States began to be associated with the idea of mass culture. As early as the 1830s, the Bowery Boys and Gals had popularized a working-class youth culture in New York based upon style, leisure time, and consumerism, but it was not until later in the century, when waves of immigration from Europe coincided with the spread of industrial capitalism, that youth began to lead the way toward the adoption of a culture of consumption and style on a national level.[18] The process of assimilation or "Americanization" was primarily the province of the young. As the children of immigrants or as immigrants themselves, they were interested in fitting into a society increasingly defined by an urban and urbane sense of style and consumerism.[19]

These teenagers and young adults usually worked to help support the family and had little leisure time or disposable income of their own, but living in the city exposed them to a world that was in stark contrast to the isolated rural homes that most of them had come from. Even young children, as historian David Nasaw has shown, often spent the bulk of their time outside on the city streets, experiencing a very different world from the one their parents had known as children, and maybe even the one their parents were living in at that moment. Young people were also influenced by the emerging culture industries of the time, such as vaudeville, touring theater groups, and, later, movie theaters. Popular culture was already being produced and packaged as entertainment. For the "children of the city," according to Nasaw, "it was not simply their spending money but their attitude toward entertainment that would actuate the final stage in the transformation of American culture from the production orientation and work ethic of a Benjamin Franklin to the consumption ethos of *Playboy* magazine."[20]

Because they were the first to embrace these changes, young people could be seen as both progressive and corrosive forces in society, and much of the debate over youth concerned this very question. Already in the first decades of the twentieth century, the brilliant critic Randolph Bourne complained about the standardizing effects of mass culture, while at the same time announcing youth as a potentially revolutionary force. Bourne argued that mass culture, film in particular, threatened to destroy all authentic folk culture, that is, all the immigrant cultures across the country. At the same time, Bourne argued that youth could and should be the leading force for social change in America.[21]

By the 1920s the link between youth and popular culture was firmly established. As mass production fed the growing hunger for consumer goods, the younger generation led a stylistic revolt against traditional mores and values. Women, feeling newly liberated by the passage of the Nineteenth Amendment, played an active role in the cultural changes, as epitomized by the flapper, the modern young woman who cast off society's norms and signaled her independence by dressing and behaving unconventionally. As images of flappers wearing short hair and short skirts were broadcast across the country, their popularity broke down patriarchal and other barriers, allowing women greater freedom in the public sphere.[22] Cultural activities began to supplant the home and school as the center of identity formation, and young people assimilated themselves—in ways their parents could not comprehend—to the new ways of a mass-cultured American society.[23] Even during the difficult years of the Great Depression and World War II, young people continued to enjoy the freedom associated with the marketplace.[24]

The effects of popular culture on American society were a subject of concern and debate long before the age of mass production and mass marketing. As early as 1835, Alexis de Tocqueville criticized American democracy for fostering undistinguished, commercialized, superficial arts that appealed to the passions rather than to taste, designed for amusement rather than cultivation. After World War II, the debate was revived. From under the dual shadows of the Nazi-controlled German media and the Hollywood film industry, the exiled German theorists Max Horkheimer and Theodor Adorno wrote critically of popular culture and the capitalist culture industries that controlled it. They compared "mass culture" to a factory, in that the "culture industries" churned out what in the theorists' view were undifferentiated, interchangeable "products" that required little of viewers and listeners in the way of engagement—the opposite of "true" art. Critics from across the ideological spectrum may have differed on the source of the problem—it was variously attributed to democracy, technology, literacy, capitalism, commodification, and American exceptionalism—but they were in general agreement that mass culture was standardized, manipulated, conservative, consumeristic, undemocratic, and inescapable, and that it had begun to replace the family and traditional venues as the agency of socialization for youth.[25]

Most troublesome to many critics in the postwar era was the discovery by the culture industries of the youth market, which resulted from the increasing disposable income available to teenagers in a period of expanding affluence. The popular products of the culture industries—films, comic books, and rock 'n' roll records—threatened to turn the young against their elders and to debase American culture in general.[26] Whether or not Elvis Presley's swiveling hips were corrupting the younger generation's morals, whether or not films such as Blackboard Jungle and Rebel without a Cause reflected or promoted juvenile delinquency, 1950s youth culture spread the idea of adolescence as a category separate from, and opposed to, adulthood.[27]

During the postwar era a number of demographic, social, and economic changes—dislocations, population mixtures, and entrepreneurial activity— forged a link between youth and the expanding culture industries. While the consumers were often fairly recently born, and newly arrived in the suburbs, the creators were other types of migrants, whether second and third generation Jews in Hollywood, or blues, folk, and country musicians, black and white, newly moved from the countryside to the cities of the Midwest.[28] The messages of the mass culture products embraced by young people often did promote the values of consumerism, over and against competing local, ethnic, and patriarchal values.[29] In fact, it was the discovery by the culture industries that, in one historian's words, "youth culture was not necessarily something to bemoan; it could be an innovation to be celebrated," which led to the juvenile delinquents of the fifties becoming the Pepsi Generation of the sixties.[30]

Social scientists and other critics who feared that the mass culture of the fifties was replacing the family and traditional venues as the agency of socialization were quite right. Rock 'n' roll, in particular, provided a way for young people to simultaneously escape from, enter into, and change the world around them. "Rock and roll was central to the white teenage experience of the 1950s," writes Wini Breines in her memoir of growing up "young, white, and miserable" in the fifties. It provided a place for "alienation, rebellion, and . . . affirmation/community."[31] Popular music "gave voice to all the warring selves inside us struggling, blindly and with a crushing sense of insecurity, to forge something resembling a coherent identity," claims another historian who came of age in the era.[32] Even the political rebellion of the New Left was often framed through popular music, first in the folk scene and then, after Bob Dylan went electric at the 1965 Newport Folk Festival, through rock music. When Barry McGuire sang, "The eastern world, it is explodin' / violence flarin', bullets loadin' / you're old enough to kill, but not for voting," and "Eve of Destruction" reached the top of the charts in 1965, it seemed as if "a mass movement of the American young was upon us."[33] Later in the decade, rock festivals literally brought the youth of the sixties together, as epitomized by the Woodstock Music and Art Fair, the legendary countercultural extravaganza in 1969 that was attended by more than 450,000 people.

Rock 'n' roll constructed the young people of the United States as a generation, in the fifties as "teenagers" and in the sixties as a "movement." From Elvis to Woodstock, youth provided the culture industries with one marketing opportunity after another. At the same time, the ideal of "youth culture" unified young people, often in opposition to mass culture. In leftist manifestos such as the Students for a Democratic Society's "Port Huron Statement" (1962) and Mario Savio's resounding speeches in the Berkeley Free Speech Movement (1964), the nascent New Left appealed to young people as both the product of the age of affluence and its potential reformers. As in previous generations, the question as to whether youth could be harnessed to bring about positive social change was hotly debated, but it seemed to be confirmed in the early years of the decade with the biracial, student-led civil rights movement. And by the Summer of Love in 1967 the hippie movement could be seen as the broader manifestation of this takeover and transformation of American culture by youth. By the end of the decade, the counterculture had in some ways become the mass culture, "a stage in the development of the values of the American middle class."[34] This is not to say simply that the youth of the sixties "sold out," but to claim that the destinies of mass culture and youth culture, long intertwined, were now identical.

The End of Youth Culture

Then, just at the moment of the ascendance of youth culture at the end of the sixties, it was over. A major downturn in the stock market and the oil embargo in 1973 resulted in a sharp increase in gas prices, long lines at the pumps, and widespread fear and anxiety. With consumer prices rising, industrial productivity declining, and unemployment growing, the deteriorating economy brought the age of abundance to an end. The fragmentation of the social movements of the 1960s, the continuing Vietnam War, the oil crisis and recession of 1973–74, and the Watergate scandal all brought about possibly the greatest distrust in government and in the possibilities for social change in American history. Politically, the forces of both power and opposition were suspect. The government, and indeed anyone who tried to claim the allegiance of the public, faced a legitimation crisis.[35]

Young people coming of age in these difficult times were no longer sure about the state of the world or their place in it. In the age of fragmentation in the 1970s there were still young people and still corporate-produced cultural products, but the categories of youth culture and mass culture lost what explanatory value they previously had. The decade opened with a slew of reports and studies on the youth of the sixties, analyzing, celebrating, and decrying the counterculture, the New Left, Black Power, Woodstock, and so on. But by the end of the decade there was no such category as "American youth."

A major part of the explanation for this transformation was that the baby boomers had come of age—with more and more of them hitting the "thirty-something" mark—and they took their dominance of the consumer economy and its culture with them into adulthood.[36] One critic suggests that adult baby boomers lived in an "age of prolonged adolescence," and behaved "more like young people."[37] The youth of the 1950s had been trained for life in a consumerist, mass culture society, and took that training, as well as their spending power, with them into adulthood. This does not mean that they never grew up, but that what had defined them as youth—whether their market position or psychological profile as "adolescent"—was no longer attributable only to a certain age group. Another critic even argues that the corporate-controlled media technology of the postwar era has brought about "the disappearance of childhood" altogether.[38] And the whole body of psychological research based upon Erik Erikson's influential theories of adolescence, which had arisen in the postwar era, had come to the conclusion that the "fixation of identity" which was supposed to occur in the teen years occurred not at all in a world driven by mass culture.[39]

In the 1950s and 1960s, the music industry usually managed to deliver the goods—music that young people could identify with and identify themselves through. By the early 1970s, however, the situation had changed. In the wake of the commercial success of Woodstock, the music business became disconnected from the youth market, too often failing to distribute the kind of music that young people could call their own. In part this was due to the collapse of the youth movement, but changes internal to the industry itself also affected the products. There were four dominant companies at the time: Columbia, Warner Brothers, Capitol, and Motown, the first three of which were major conglomerates. In 1973, David Geffen sold the independent Asylum Records to Warner Brothers for $7 million. By the end of that year, eight out of the ten firms with records on Billboard's "Hot 100" were "diversified corporations with major holdings in industries other than recorded music."[40] The majors controlled the market by "buying the contracts of established artists and buying once independent companies," effectively making it too expensive for independents to compete.[41] Economies of scale gave the majors an advantage not only in production but also, and especially, in advertising and access to the retail chains.

In always looking for the next big thing, and through the process of consolidation within the industry, the music business and music itself had become tame. There was little incentive for the major labels to seek out new music, and little room for new artists to break into the market. But the three sounds that dominated the seventies—country/folk rock, progressive rock, and disco—too often sounded impersonal to those who sought a sense of identification through music. The ideal of youth culture might have faded, but the power of rock 'n' roll had not: young people still craved "the magic that can set you free."[42] Those who could not embrace the "peaceful, easy feeling" of commercial music would have to look to the margins of the music business for the magic. And in order to find that music, they would have to make it and distribute it themselves.

DIY

"Here's three chords, now form a band" proffered London's *Sniffin Glue* fanzine—a perfect articulation of the do-it-yourself (DIY) ethos of punk. DIY provides a key to understanding the origins and evolution of punk and its relationship to the sixties. Sociologist Stephen Duncombe defines DIY as "at once a critique of the dominant mode of passive consumer culture and something far more important: the active creation of an alternative culture."[43] But the implications of DIY can cut at least two ways: DIY can be a way to opt out, or a method of transformation of the dominant culture. The first punks in Los Angeles straddled the two, ambivalent about their relationship with the dominant culture. Later postsuburban hardcore punks rejected explicitly any interaction with the dominant culture.

The DIY ethos attracted young people to punk because of its musical implications. Once only professionals and technocrats could make rock music, but DIY let all fans become active participants. As Falling James, a high school student in L.A. in the seventies, remarked upon seeing punk for the first time, "If they can do that, I can do it."[44] Like countless others, he picked up the guitar and formed a band immediately. There were many ways to build a scene through the DIY ethos, such as publishing a zine or even just dressing punk, in addition to making music. While the idea of doing it yourself was not unique to punk, drawing on postwar youth culture traditions such as fan clubs, rock newsletters, and radical political bulletins and magazines, the transformation of this ethos reflected the general transformation in youth from the sixties to the seventies to the eighties.

Greg Shaw and Suzy Shaw, his wife.
© Jenny Lens Punk Archive/Cache Agency.

An important model for Southern California punks was Greg Shaw's *Bomp! Magazine*, one of the first zines to pay attention to punk. Shaw, whose record store hosted The Damned visit in April 1977, was a fanatic about rock 'n' roll, who as a seventeen-year-old had headed out to the blossoming Haight–Ashbury in 1966 in search of the latest thing in rock, the psychedelic sound and scene of the Grateful Dead, Janis Joplin, and the Jefferson Airplane. There he published the first San Francisco-based rock 'n' roll magazine, *Mojo-Navigator Rock & Roll News*. As he remembered, "The music scene was just getting started. The obvious way to get involved with what was happening was to start a zine. I had the background. I had a mimeograph machine, I'd been in science fiction fandom, I knew how to edit and publish a magazine. That was *Mojo*."[45] *Mojo-Navigator*, after *Crawdaddy!* out of Cambridge, Massachusetts, was the second American rock 'n' roll zine—an independently published magazine dedicated not only to supporting a rock scene but also to creating one. Cranked out by hand on Shaw's mimeograph machine, the zine mixed fandom with an active participation in the creation of rock culture, eventually becoming a model for Jann Wenner's *Rolling Stone*.

After *Mojo* folded in 1968 Shaw moved to Los Angeles and in 1970 started *Bomp!,* another mimeo zine. Shaw helped establish a national, even international, network of rock 'n' roll fanatics, maintaining a mailing list of thousands of fellow devotees of underground rock. "A scene began to grow around it. Those were the days, 1970 to '72, when rock 'n' roll was lame; there was nothing really happening. Those of us who cared gathered around these little campfires and *Bomp!* was one of them."[46] *Bomp!* was established in explicit rejection of what *Rolling Stone* had already become—a symbol to Shaw of the corporate infiltration of rock 'n' roll.

For Shaw and his ilk, the guiding premise was that there was great rock 'n' roll being made, it just wasn't being heard. To them, for brief moments in the fifties and the sixties the great rockers had received mass distribution through the record companies and radio. By the early seventies, Shaw found barely anything worthwhile on the radio or in the bins of the record store chains, and he spent his time searching for obscure rock recordings from earlier eras and for the new bands that he believed were continuing the spirit in spite of record company apathy. "Music is becoming an investment industry," Shaw argued in 1978. "Real rock 'n' roll is wild experimentation and letting new ideas go crazy and then seeing how they do."[47] Shaw still believed in the power of rock 'n' roll to unify youth culture, as well as the power of this youth culture to change the world. He attempted to bring forth from the sixties the rebellious, underground spirit that he had experienced in the Haight–Ashbury: "My standards of teen culture were set at a time when teen culture ruled the world, where people were creating for themselves and were not dictated to by huge corporations."[48] While Shaw might have underestimated the corporate influence in sixties rock, the conclusions he drew led him to retain the ideals which had brought him to rock fandom in the first place.

Shaw and fans like him were not necessarily anticapitalist, nor anti-mass culture, but they went underground because of the lack of mainstream interest in what they saw as real rock 'n' roll. Further, the experience of "underground culture" created the opportunity for "involvement in a creative experience" that the passive experience of consumption denied to youth: "The best culture is one that involves everybody, it's participatory. . . . You are not a passive consumer."[49]

For Shaw and friends, rock 'n' roll—real rock 'n' roll, true rock 'n' roll, however they defined it—provided the impetus and center to the creative experience that defined the underground culture. As Lisa Fancher, who came in from the Valley to work for Shaw at *Bomp!* as a sixteen-year-old in 1975, and later started her own fanzine *Biff! Bang! Pow!,* wrote in a letter to a New York fanzine: "I've gone through 'above-ground' jobs like the L.A. TIMES, SOUNDS, RECORD MIRROR real fast because I'm not willing to write about anything or take bullshit from various editors who know absolutely NOTHING about Rock & Roll, but [only] about being industry peons." Fancher, like Shaw, established her identity through her opposition to the music business and by her willingness to sacrifice anything to save the soul of rock 'n' roll for the future: "See I have a real idealistic, MORAL philosophy toward future rockers. I feel bad they have to listen to the things they do on the radio and read the things they do in CIRCUS [a mainstream rock fan magazine]. I don't hate them or think they're stupid—we haven't done our job in getting the alternatives to them."[50]

Fans like Fancher and Shaw believed they had to take it upon themselves to do the hard work necessary—starting their own zines, writing letters to other diehard fans around the globe—in order to save the spirit of rock 'n' roll and deliver it to the youth of America and the world. Involvement in the underground culture meant, in part, proselytizing to those who had no other access to the underground, who were thus isolated and captive to the industry. Shaw argued, "I really believe that we have to get to the masses. . . . I can't believe that kids are such sheep that they will buy anything stuffed down their throats by the companies."[51] In response to the bleak prospects for good music reaching the public, Shaw became a record producer, retaining a faith in the ability of youth to choose real rock if given the opportunity.

Shaw formed Bomp Records only because the bands he liked couldn't get signed by the major labels. Bomp, he later claimed, was the first truly independent record label for rock music in the country, with no ties to any of the major labels or distributors.[52] Bomp pressed one thousand copies of a single by the Flamin' Groovies in 1974, distributing them all through mail order in the absence of any other network for national independent record distribution. Over the next few years Bomp released singles by Beatles-influenced cult bands, an album by Iggy Pop, and compilations of garage rock bands from the sixties in the *Pebbles* series. Shaw and others embraced a do-it-yourself ethic as an alternative way of realizing the older ideals of youth culture and mass culture, not as a rejection of them. Their goal was to create an inclusive youth culture based on rock 'n' roll.

The first punks in Los Angeles, however, were not quite as hopeful or idealistic as Shaw, although they did not reject outright—at least not initially—the possibilities of harnessing mass culture and youth culture to their own ends. L.A. punks were more interested in establishing terms of distinction for themselves. And Los Angeles punks defined distinction aesthetically, by the style of dress and the sound of the music. From the beginning, performance was key to the L.A. punk aesthetic and ideology. While many of the first people attracted to punk in L.A. came from the tiny rock underground, many of those had been attracted to rock 'n' roll, especially glam, for its theatricality. Further, if these rockers had attempted to resurrect the rock 'n' roll spirit, much of that spirit concerned attitude rather than technical proficiency. Finally, a significant section of the new punk scene came to punk not only for the music, in pursuit of a revitalized rock 'n' roll, but for an outlet for artistic expression—members of the Weirdos and Screamers, for example, had been artists before becoming punks, and there was considerable crossover in attendance at performance art and punk shows in Los Angeles.[53] From the beginning, L.A. punk rested on a number of unstable contradictions, reflected in the use of the DIY ethos as both an extension and a rejection of sixties idealism.

"Forming"

Many of the first self-proclaimed punks L.A. punks were old enough to remember the music of the sixties and its ideals, but were less sanguine about their place in society and dissatisfied with the outcome of the previous decade's youth movements and rock revival. *Slash* magazine typified the tension within the scene as to whether punk was intended as a revolution *within* the system or a revolution *against* it. Some punks hoped that punk would destroy rock 'n' roll and the music business in its current incarnation, while others saw punk as the next big thing that would sweep the industry. Most punks oscillated between these two positions. Punks were allowed to waver because at least two positions were available; that is, punks were not dependent on the major labels to spread their music, they could do it themselves.

And *Slash* wasn't the only voice defining the punk scene, as more and more punks throughout the region began to publish and distribute their own zines. Writing and circulating a zine was one way to be a punk, as valid as being in a band. Each zine had a clubby, insider tone to it; but as a group, they represent a broad range of interests and desires. Phast Phreddie Patterson's *Back Door Man* (published from Torrance), *I Wanna Be Your Dog* (from Hollywood and Paris), and *Raw Power* (from Woodland Hills) were all rock fanzines that covered punk as part of their search for the latest best thing. And a slew of gossipy, excited xerox zines emerged to participate as insiders in the punk scene. *Generation X* came out of Hollywood in 1977, edited by Jade Zebest and Zandra. *Lobotomy: the brainless magazine*, "produced and directed by Pleasant and Randy Detroit" arrived in late 1977 from Beverly Hills. *The Panic*, put out by Diana and Michelle, started in June 1978. And Joanne K. and friends produced *Nihil Opinionated Magazine* in 1978. *Flipside*—created by four Whittier High School grads, and destined to be the most influential on the later hardcore scenes—came out with its first issue just after *Slash*'s May 1977 debut.

While *Slash* was a professionally (though cheaply) printed four-color tabloid-size magazine, most zines were typed and handwritten, photocopied, folded, and stapled by punks, with a printing of anywhere from twenty to one hundred copies. Punks distributed them at shows, at Shaw's Bomp Records and a few other record stores, and through the mail. Zine writers discussed a range of issues and events from local shows and gossip to international punk recordings and happenings, to diatribes and manifestos on the meaning of punk. They covered and helped to create a punk scene that was largely ignored, if not reviled, in the commercial media.

The major record companies showed no interest in L.A. punk. They had seen what the Sex Pistols had done in England—where the band had been signed and dumped by two major record labels before recording a note—and they assumed punk was a British thing that would never catch on in the United States. One of the Weirdos told *Flipside* in 1977, "There's so much shit that the industry's produced. Just listen to the radio and it all sounds pretty much the same. For me and the guys in the band, it's more a revolt against all this boring shit. Even with all the stuff that's out, the radio still does the same thing. There's nothing fresh—nothing new. All the industry does is take a lot of money and make something real slick—over and over again."[54] Driven, then, by necessity, L.A. punks and fellow-travelers—usually older people (mid- to late-twenties) who had accumulated a few hundred dollars of savings and a smattering of recording equipment—began committing their artistic output to vinyl through fledgling independent record labels.

Punks didn't need corporate support, for by the middle of the 1970s it was possible, with a minor capital outlay, to record a couple of songs on a four-track recorder in a garage or jerry-rigged studio, press the recording into a 45-rpm single, print up a black-and-white sleeve, and sell several hundred copies at punk shows and through local record stores on consignment. For his first single, Tito Larriva of the Plugz borrowed a thousand dollars from his father. Selling the seven-inch record from the trunk of his car at local shows, he recovered his costs within weeks. The Plugz then recorded their first album live in the studio (with no overdubs) and released it on their own label. Robbie Fields recorded some of the suburban bands for his Posh Boy label, releasing a live album by F-Word in 1978. Dangerhouse, What?, and Upsetter Records, all formed by twenty-something punks, released records by local punk bands in 1978 and 1979. The founders of *Slash* established a record label, releasing singles and albums by local bands such as the Germs, X, and the Flesh Eaters. Since they were played almost instantly on "Rodney on the Roq" on Sunday nights, these recordings made punk accessible throughout the region to those who could not make it all the way into Hollywood on a Saturday night. Thus, while the motives behind the do-it-yourself punk movement were mostly musical initially, at least in Los Angeles, the results made both the music and the ethos more widely available.

The do-it-yourself ethos produced a particular aesthetic within L.A. punk. As early as July 1977 Chris Ashford had released L.A. punk's first single, on his new What? Records, a two-track recording of "Forming," by the Germs, backed with a live version of "Sex Boy." On "Forming," recorded in guitarist Pat Smear's mother's garage, punk aesthetics and punk technology meet, as Bobby Pyn sings,

Rip them down
hold me up
tell them that
I'm your gun
Pull my trigger
I am bigger thaaannnn

through the right channel, while all the musical tracks come through the left speaker. Then, after singing the verses and chorus, Pyn rants in whiny monotone, "Whoever would buy this shit is a fuckin' jerk, he's playing it all wrong, the drums are too slow, the bass is too fast, the chords are wrong, he's making the ending too long . . . ah quit," and then the vocal track cuts out with an audible buzz in the right channel as the musicians finish off the song. The b-side, "Sex Boy," recorded surreptitiously at the Germs' audition for a Cheech & Chong movie, sounds even worse, as you can hear people talking and bottles breaking over the sound of the music.[55] As the *Flipside* reviewer wrote, "I think this little, lousey [*sic*] shitty piece of vinyl, has got to be the best thing Bomp has ever stocked in the singles section. I mean, it's the last name in raunchy. . . . I mean, it's so shitty. It's mastered lousy."[56] Rodney Bingenheimer thought the record was "very well produced": "That's the sound everybody else is looking for, the garage sound."[57]

The record captured the aesthetic of the L.A. version of the punk revolution, but, despite what Rodney said, in 1977 it was a sound only the committed could appreciate.

3 MESSAGE from the UNDERWORLD

Punk, Power Pop, and New Wave

The day after the Sex Pistols played the Winterland, L.A. punks returned home to discover that the Masque had been shut down by the fire marshall for numerous code violations. The following month, seventeen bands came together to stage a benefit concert for the club at the Elks Lodge in downtown L.A., raising $4,300 for the legal fees Mullen needed to fight the landlord's eviction proceedings. Whereas less than a year earlier there had been no club for punk and no scene to speak of, and maybe not even one person in L.A. who called him- or herself a punk, and the only live rock 'n' roll was being played by pop, proto-punk bands such as the Motels, the Pop!, and the Dogs or by unsigned heavy metal arena rock wannabees Van Halen and Quiet Riot, now, over two consecutive nights, punk bands of various stripes gathered to showcase the talents of the L.A. scene.[1]

Musically, the scene was quickly maturing. The deans of L.A. punk—the post-teenage nihilist, Day-Glo pogoers the Weirdos, and the Screamers, with their multimedia "synth hysteria" led by hypnotic frontman Tomata Du Plenty—headlined the two nights.[2] Exene Cervenka of X performed in her diamond tiara, stretch pants, and boxing gloves. Bruce Barf of the Skulls pissed over the balcony. Malcolm McLaren, the Sex Pistols' Svengali, made the rounds. *Slash*'s photographer hung out in the men's room taking "punk potty photos" of punks with their pants down. Audio and video recording crews were scampering about, including a film crew from

Tokyo. Punks in dog collars, chains, and spiked hair posed on the massive lobby stairway, wandered down back halls searching for dark rooms, and pogoed and careened among other punks and others checking out the scene. All this in a beautiful if slightly run-down ballroom in the enormous Elks Lodge across from MacArthur Park.

The shows were big enough news in L.A. to warrant two articles in the *Los Angeles Times*. "While still too primitive for most tastes," wrote Kristine McKenna in a short review of the Friday night performances, "the best of these bands offer a valid, if inconsistent alternative to slick mainstream rock product."[3] In a longer overview titled "A Positive Perspective on Punk," Robert Hilburn, the *Times*' pop music majordomo, approvingly cited Mullen's attempt "to demonstrate that the L.A. punk scene is a positive, rather than negative social and musical force. However aggressive some of the bands and rambunctious some of the audience, the overriding spirit is one of fun."[4] Hilburn had written about New York punk in the past, calling it "a colorful, invigorating alternative to the smooth polished approach that has characterized pop music in recent years," but this was his first acknowledgment of the local scene.[5] L.A. punk was achieving some respectability.

When it came to the music, however, the *Times*' critics were not yet hearing what many in the audience heard. Punks tended to reject outsiders' standards of musicality, but by February 1978, more punk bands were closer to meeting those very standards. To some extent, it was a question of proficiency. Punk bands had now been rehearsing and performing for several months; even the Germs occasionally managed to play a song that actually sounded something like music to more traditional ears. But Hilburn was still not impressed. After the Masque benefit show, he wrote, "The X band was mostly routine."[6] The fans, however, knew that something new was going on musically. *Slash* described that same performance as having propelled X "in one night . . . from cult status to front-line contender." "Maybe one of the most hardcore bands of the area, they offer the most straightforward no bullshit punk noise I've heard in a while," the *Slash* critic wrote. "X are uncompromising and uneasy listening, routine they are not. The punks know. Too bad for the others."[7] In the same issue was a review of an X performance the following week at the Whisky a Go-Go: "X have become one of the most exciting groups around in a matter of weeks, and if this show is any indication they're soon going to leave

Exene Cervenka of X with Billy Zoom (left) and D.J. Bonebrake (on drums), 1980.
© Jenny Lens Punk Archive/Cache Agency.

everyone else way behind. To watch John Doe screaming his song into the mike, all contorted with passion while Exene is shaking in trance behind and Billy Zoom is grinning insanely while hitting his guitar; to watch Exene and John trading vocals while the music literally sizzles and burns right thru you is something you're not about to forget. The intensity and originality of their tunes is amazing."[8]

While Hilburn did not yet see or hear it, X's music appealed to a wider spectrum of the L.A. audience than the art-initiated, giving voice to the rootlessness of postmodern life, and particularly of car-mad L.A. X's sound and lyrics, and punk more generally in Los Angeles, reflected its locale. The cultural critic Greil Marcus, one of the earliest to assess

John Doe of X, 1980.
© Jenny Lens Punk Archive/ Cache Agency.

punk's place in what he called "the secret history of the twentieth century," claimed that British punk made a fissure—"a precious disruption . . . almost transcendentally odd"—in the everyday life not only of punks, but of the world. Punk was possibly of world historical importance not because it transformed the record industry, or brought about an organized youth rebellion, but because in a world where nothing seemed to happen, one could see and hear punk and think, "this is actually happening." "The Sex Pistols made a breach in the pop milieu . . . [that] opened into the realm of everyday life," calling into question all social facts, everything that everyone could take for granted: "Judged according to its demands on the world, a Sex Pistols record had to change the way a given person performed his or her commute—which is to say that the record had to connect that act to every other, and then call the enterprise as a whole into question. Thus would the record change the world."[9] L.A. punk made a similar "precious disruption," at least on the individual level for individual young people in Southern California, mixing the Situationist-inspired antics of London punks with the noir version of Los Angeles that dominated the subcultural vision of the city at least since Raymond Chandler's private eye Philip Marlowe roamed the streets. Young people created a punk rock specifically suited for the cultural and social environment of Los Angeles—and this vision was enticing to many people across the landscape, not just those who looked to rock or art for their identity.

Combining fragments of local depictions produced by the likes of Chandler, Joan Didion, Charles Bukowski, Nathanael West, and Kenneth Anger, with older, urban, European, bohemian influences like Arthur Rimbaud and Charles Baudelaire, the first L.A. punks attempted to erase their pasts, constructing themselves anew in the manner of previous urban youth subcultures. Where they originally came from was unimportant, as they rechristened themselves and created a new vision of their city and their world, rejecting the sunshine and surf. Even as they had come to L.A. from the East Coast to find something to do, John Doe and Exene of X sang,

> She had to leave Los Angeles
> She had started to hate every nigger and jew
> Every mexican who gave her a lot of shit
> Every homosexual and the idle rich.

In response to this vision, more and more young people across the region were finding their way to punk, and L.A. punk was representing a greater range of perspectives. At the Elks Lodge benefit there was still room for the Day-Glo and trash bag aesthetic of the Weirdos and the Screamers, there was still a place for the licorice whips and peanut butter and body slashing of the Germs, but the artistic focus was expanding. Though the punk rock performed at the Elks Lodge shows did sound different from anything traditional rock critics were used to, it was sounding good to more and more people. The aesthetics of distinction still marked a line between subculture and dominant culture, but as more people came in contact with the subculture they began to hear what the early punks heard, even if the critics still did not.

As the music changed, so did the composition of the crowd listening to it. If the *Times* was curious enough to send two critics, hundreds of others from the greater Los Angeles area were curious too. "Many new faces, the legions are growing (on weekends anyway)," noted a *Slash* reporter. "Healthy high school girlies very self-consciously safety-pinned from head to toe. In the back of the main room there is hair everywhere on the floor. Someone got clipped right on the spot. A case of instant conversion, I guess."[10] Instant conversion or ritual sacrifice? The L.A. scene was rife with tales of "hippies" forcibly transformed into punks at shows. All it took was a couple people to hold one down and another to wield the scissors. But did this mean that the hippie was now a punk? Or was he still really a hippie, only now with short hair? At some point, every punk had had the conversion experience: "This is actually happening and I want in." But once you were in, you had to decide what to make of those who came in after you. Was the punk revolution under way? Or was it nothing more than an invasion by the mindless masses?

Slash expressed ambivalence about whether newcomers should be welcomed into the fold. In many ways, the scene provided a surrogate family; as one punk recalled, "I'd fall into this group of pogoers, and they would pick me up immediately. It was a group of fifty kids and they were very nice and gentle."[11] At the same time, as *Times* critic Kristine McKenna remembered, "I went to shows for two years and no one would say a word to me."[12] Ah, but that was because she was a *Los Angeles Times* critic—and therefore she could not be a "real" punk.

"The new punk testament"

The Elks Lodge shows occurred at a pivotal moment for the L.A. scene. Throughout the year, the main topics of debate in the correspondence section of *Slash* were the elitist attitudes of the Hollywood punk insiders, and by extension, the meaning of punk—two questions inextricably linked in the search for subcultural capital. *Slash* defended both elitism and openness, reflecting its ambivalence about punk, youth culture, and mass culture. It set itself up as the voice of punk, promoting the "New

Punk Testament," yet debated over the meaning of punk—debate often scandalous and slanderous, but open nonetheless. Claude Bessy readily published letters attacking him, Mullen, and other insiders, then gave his pen free reign in responding with wit, fury, and a raging vocabulary. As Kickboy Face, Bessy denied the elitism of L.A. punk. In response to a letter in May 1978, he wrote: "that 'clique' you mention is actually 5 or 6 cliques, each one more 'punk' than the other one, all of them wasting their time and energy at their silly games. You could start one yourself (all you need is 5 to 10 really bored people) and feel on top of things!"[13]—an easy enough claim for him to make, as he already had his turf staked out, but also partly true.

Within the pages of the zine, Kickboy Face always won the arguments, as he was the best writer and had the last word. But there were many within the punk scene who would not be cowed into submission by his vitriol. And as new people joined the scene, they continued to redefine punk according to their desires. So they debated the meaning of punk. Should power pop be included? Should punks hate the rich? Were L.A. punks holier than thou? Were safety pins currently out of vogue? And always the matter of hair, hair, hair.

Many of the people who participated in the punk scene may not have called themselves punks, but they kept coming back to the shows, they kept reading the zines, and listening to the records. Punk was the only thing going on at the time, and it made sense—maybe not all of it, but enough to draw those looking for something to do. The Hollywood scene was open to newcomers who dressed in variety of ways with a variety of haircuts, as photos from the period attest. "Committed" punks may have called the guys with long hair "poseurs" or "weekend punks," but, in fact, punk identity remained in flux. Most who were attracted to punk were not sure what it was, and while they knew that long hair was not punk, that negative knowledge did not give them enough to go on. So you cut your hair—willingly or not—then what? How to create a positive identity out of punk was either uncertain or uncodified.

"A few la-la-la's won't kill you"

One contradiction that created tension within the punk scene revolved around the question of how much of rock 'n' roll should be taken as a model, or at least as part of punk's heritage. Was Elvis a punk? Was Rimbaud? Groucho Marx? Who were the proper ancestors to today's punks in Hollywood?[14] Because there was no musical definition of punk, lovers of rock 'n' roll were free to see punk as merely an extension of this tradition. Early on in L.A., the term "punk" was used almost interchangeably with "New Wave," especially by critics such as Robert Hilburn, but also by scenesters themselves. A skinny tie with a red sharkskin suit was as much a punk outfit as a spiked dog collar and plastic trash bag dress.Djs in clubs mixed punk with New Wave and reggae, anything that sounded different from rock radio, as there was so little punk vinyl to play between sets. Punk bands like the Go-Gos, the Alleycats, and the Flyboys, who came up through the L.A. punk scene, sounded rough at first, but, as they improved technically and refined their sound, paid homage to fifties and sixties pop rock styles, partly to make their music more accessible. The scene accommodated a great variety of musical styles, though most were louder, cruder, maybe faster versions of the basic rock 'n' roll sound.

As the scene grew, "punk" and "New Wave" came to signify distinct musical styles, fashions, and ideologies. Punk became three-chord rock, hard and up-tempo, descended from the Ramones, who defined the genre. New Wave became the poppier side of punk, with bouncy rhythms, often tinged with Farfisa organ or horns or synthesizer. By 1978, the pages of *Slash*, and the scene as a whole, were filled with debates about what constituted true punk music, as well as true punk behavior and politics. One particularly acrimonious debate flared up between Brendan Mullen and Greg Shaw. Shaw started Bomp Records in part because he was fascinated with the garage bands of the sixties, a sound that by the mid-seventies had evolved into what was fairly accurately called power pop. To Shaw and his fellow record collectors and almost obsessive aficionados, punk rock fit nicely into the path he had been following for a decade. But to punks more recently arrived to underground music fandom, the music and the man were suspect, too retrograde, too New Wave, not punk enough.

In early 1978, after an interview with Shaw had been published in the January issue of *Slash*, he was viciously slammed in letters to the zine.[15] One letter-writer called power pop "adolescent, high-pitched whine coated with sugar" and "moronic schmaltz."[16] Brendan Mullen wrote, "Powerpop is not the only logical progression of 'punk rock' to more tonal and melodic adaptedness. It's only a cop-out from a consciousness which could eventually create something different."[17] Clearly there was more than music at stake here. Shaw responded by first laying out his credentials: "I've loved good rock & roll all my life. I was buying records by Elvis and Chuck Berry when I was 6, I was disgusted when the music died in the early '60s, I lived through the years of pop mania in the '60s and at all times my life was dedicated to finding or helping create more of the highest quality rock & roll music."Having established his bona fides as a rocker, Shaw reminded his readers that he, too, had slogged through the wasteland of seventies culture, "the years of James Taylor and John Denver." He claimed credit for his own role in laying the foundation for punk: "I don't think there would be any punk scene today if people like me, during those years, hadn't invented fanzines, underground records, etc., and promoted awareness of the '60s punk groups that were the direct inspiration of all of today's SLASH idols."[18]

Shaw pleaded for tolerance, for an inclusiveness within punk for a variety of musical forms: "Enough already with posing and posturing and rhetoric and fucking dialectical dogma. We all just wanna have some fun, and we're in this together to make the scene happen. As long as the music is coming from the people and relates honestly to its audience, it's New Wave and that's all I'm interested in promoting or protecting." To Shaw, punks' search for differentiation and distinction was destroying the music's potential. His fight with Mullen boiled down to a simple stylistic issue: "A few la-la-la's won't kill you."

The fight between power pop and punk was ironic because power pop was the acknowledged local musical forebear of L.A. punk. In the days before punk emerged in the city, bands like the Motels, the Pop!, and the Last had displayed the only signs of live musical vitality.[19] And, in fact, Shaw was not arguing that power pop should replace punk, nor that it truly was punk, only that it should be allowed to exist alongside punk, under the rubric "New Wave," as the commercial alternative to a punk music which "should remain underground if it is to remain pure." Punk "could survive indefinitely, as the conscience of rock & roll and as an experimental medium," while power pop could take over the airwaves so that at least the people for whom punk was too negative or inaccessible could hear good music. Shaw rejected accusations that he promoted power pop for his own commercial objectives: "I am obsessed—as I've always been—with great music, and there's never enough to satisfy me. I want to see the entire world obsessed with rock & roll mania and all its cultural byproducts."[20]

Therein lay the problem, however. As more of the world took notice of punk, more of the older punks wanted everyone else to go away. Kickboy Face still rejected the idea that punk should be a "secret club," arguing, "If our sound stays a cult matter it's going to die and life will once again be a very sad ordeal."[21] But after this debate, it became clear that punk had to be redefined more explicitly. Shaw showed his sixties roots in his faith that the softer side of punk rock, not the "ugly, negative and violent" side, could provide the basis for a "lasting youth culture and a musical genre that will reach and change the lives of millions."

The creation of a "lasting youth culture" was not, however, the punk revolution most *Slash* writers were seeking. And *Slash* and Mullen were not really sure that they wanted to "reach and change the lives of millions." So they rejected the music of such descendants of the proto-punk popsters as the Last, the Motels, and the Quick. They were ambivalent about the possibility and desirability of using punk as a vehicle for the youth culture transformation of mass culture. And Shaw's embracing of the DIY ethic—which could have qualified him as a punk—disqualified him in its unabashed advocacy of such "hippie" values as community and youth culture. The debate fractured the scene almost down the middle and extended far beyond the pages of *Slash*.[22]

The question was not only one of musical taste and internecine struggles for subcultural capital; it became inevitably one of money as well. The lure of the New Wave was as much a commercial proposition as a musical one. As punk gained a degree of attention and notoriety—nationally after the Sex Pistols' Winterland gig in January 1978, and locally after the Elks Lodge shows—not only was the definition of punk potentially up for grabs, with more people involved, but L.A. punk became a potentially viable commodity. A year before, Mullen could have tolerated power pop and New Wave as loosely defined genres within the general punk revolution, but now they began to represent if not yet the corporate product, certainly the softer edge of the revolution, maybe even the reactionary backlash.

Even if Shaw, himself, was not out to exploit the scene, others like Kim Fowley, who staged a series of "New Wave Nights" at the Whisky when the term "New Wave" still had a broader meaning, were unabashedly in it with the traditional motives of a rock 'n' roll promoter. At earlier times, punks had been grateful for the opportunity to perform and see bands, and thus looked past the seedier side of Fowley's personality and ambition. Now he was accused of trying to profit from the scene. Which, of course, he was.[23]

Rodney Bingenheimer was perhaps even more emblematic of the difficulty of drawing a line between punk and New Wave, between art and commerce, between the revolutionary and the reactionary. When he began his radio show on KROQ, he played mostly New York bands and imports; it was the only place on L.A. radio to find the Ramones and the Sex Pistols. As he claimed in early 1978, "I sort of started this scene 'cos who was doing this a year and a half ago? Nobody else was. I was on the radio." But maybe because of his too-glam rooster haircut, or his tendency to hang out in the corner booth of the Whisky—where he occasionally booked acts—with the most glamorous of rockers and wannabee models; maybe because his show, although relegated to just two hours on Sunday nights, was broadcast over a mainstream (if small) rock station; or maybe because he had the show, which made him seem powerful to others—whatever the reasons, Rodney was as much vilified as celebrated throughout the scene. He was accused simultaneously of ignoring L.A. bands and of raking in the dough from L.A. punk. He denied the charges continually, arguing, "So, what do these kids want from me? I'm doing the best I can do, it's only two hours. They say I should play L.A. bands—they don't have records, how do you play invisible records? The L.A. bands that do have records, they should turn 'em up or something in the studio."[24] He was not even paid for the privilege of taking to the airwaves once a week. But some resented Rodney's attitude and "power," as the Angry Samoans expressed in the nasty "Get Off the Air":

> You pathetic male groupie
> You don't impress me
> Get off the air, you fuckin' square
> You're just a jerk as far as I can see.[25]

The distinction between punk and New Wave became more important in 1978 because, as the world paid more attention to the music, more money was at stake. When the Dickies became the first L.A. punk band to sign to a major label, releasing a single on A&M in 1978, punks celebrated, but wondered if maybe the Dickies' humorous approach to punk was lost on the mainstream world. In the context of the music of the period, their sound was truly radical—they were possibly the fastest band on the planet—but politically they could be seen as tame. The joke was too arch, too goofy, so that their cover versions of Black Sabbath's "Paranoia" and Barry McGuire's "Eve of Destruction," songs with dark messages, blended smoothly and humorously with their renditions of Boyce and Hart's "She" and the Banana Splits theme song "The Tra La La Song." This is not to say they were "New Wave" and not "punk," but of all the L.A. punk bands, this was the one that A&M Records chose to take a chance on (a wager that never paid off in the United States).

While the Elks Lodge concert in February may not have won over the masses or the *Los Angeles Times* critics, it was instrumental in converting bored teenagers and twentysomethings. As one writer captured the moment, "The punks' livid music, raging lyrics, and ragtag fashions would not—could not—be ignored henceforth. The days of '100 punks rule' were closing, and ever-growing numbers of the curious and the strange were being pulled into the music's blaring maelstrom."[26]

Neither those "100 punks" nor Craig Lee's "Hollywood 50" ever dominated the scene in exactly the way they would have liked to, and they never policed the borders rigorously or effectively. At punk shows, who was in the "in-crowd" was never clear, and was largely a result of self-definition. If you found your crowd and declared it "in," then it was in, Bessy argued. If you didn't, and you saw another crowd that looked "in," then you could define yourself as "out"—and that could be either a good or bad thing. But the distinction between insiders and outsiders was never rigid. Because much of the scene was made up of "outsiders"—those who saw themselves as separate from and often opposed to the "straight" world— there was never a clear sense of insider status at punk rock shows in L.A. Most people on the scene were not true scenesters, and many did not want to be. While a central cabal could be identified by focusing on *Slash*, the Masque, and a few of the bands, locales, and institutions, the environment was never hermetic; there were too many openings to outsiders. To some extent, this was a consequence of punk ideology and aesthetic, and of the particular L.A. variant as it developed: if anyone could do it, anyone *would* do it.

Early on in L.A., if you were there, you were a punk, more or less. The scene was not completely open; a certain elitism reigned. But it was an elitism of the outcasts, the losers, the geeks. You didn't have to be a star, or even have friends among the scenesters; not enough people came out on any given night to make the issue of definitions much of a problem. The punk identity was still developing. Even longhairs circulated relatively freely. Every once in a while they would find themselves with a haircut— sometimes voluntarily, sometimes not—but usually they were left alone.[27] Many of the people who participated in the punk scene may not have called themselves punks, but they kept coming back. It was the only thing going on at the time, and it made sense. Maybe not all of it, but enough of it to draw the curious and adventurous over and over again.

One example of a nonpunk punk was Richard Meltzer. Poet, rock critic, sometime lyric writer for Blue Oyster Cult ("I'm burnin', I'm burnin', I'm burnin' for you"), sometime faux sociologist (*The Aesthetics of Rock)*, he was a figure right out of the late-sixties, early-seventies beatnik under-ground, part Charles Bukowski, part Lester Bangs. Like so many, he was drawn to punk not because he was a punk by any strict definition, but because this was where something was happening. And if it was center-ing around music, then Meltzer would bang on a keyboard—easier even than a guitar for hiding his lack of musicianship—and sing songs in front of his friends. His band, Vom (as in vomit), was barely a band at all, really a joke, but the same thing could be said about a lot of the punk bands, as that was what punk was about. Punks despised him because his punk critique was aimed at punk itself. Meltzer was, Kickboy Face declared, a "failed philosopher but highly successful con man."[28]

So maybe Meltzer wasn't a punk, and the world may be a better place because his band survived only eight miserable performances. But he did have a Pacifica radio show, "Hepcats from Hell," on which he played punk. Still, he was too old (born in 1945), he had come up through the rock counterculture of the sixties, and had too many connections to its past, which was by now thoroughly discredited. But if Meltzer wasn't a punk according to your standards, or mine, or those of Kickboy Face, he did know this was the only thing going on in "Endless Summerville."[29] And without a definition of punk that would hold, punk would continue to attract too many people—people who would make of it what they wanted.

Richard Meltzer,
July 1977.
© Jenny Lens Punk
Archive/Cache
Agency.

The Scene

The scene was becoming amorphous and uncontainable, rife with tensions and conflicts. It could be defined at any given moment, but the definition stuck only for that moment, and only for the interested parties. Was punk something completely new, something that no one outside could possibly understand? Or was it the latest manifestation of artistic or teenage or political rebellion? The Hollywood punk scene had begun with a close connection to the sixties. Many of the twentysomething scenesters had had long hair, and some were old enough to have had direct experience with earlier counterculture and its associated philosophies. It was this history that accounted for much of the more overtly political content in early L.A. punk, such as it existed. But that history was distrusted by newer and younger punks, for whom the past had no resonance whatsoever. Elders like Greg Shaw, Kim Fowley, and Rodney Bingenheimer were increasingly viewed as suspect, tainted by their attachment to music life before punk.

The lines hardened when other voices emerged to stake a claim on punk. If Shaw's definition ultimately lost out, drowned by the more vitriolic and splenetic pens of Bessy and Mullen, Shaw himself did not disappear. His vision was attractive to others, he continued to reach them through his Bomp Records, and he provided an important model for how to survive outside not only the mainstream music business but also the hip Hollywood scene. Similarly, Bingenheimer was never ostracized from the Hollywood clique, but he became less relevant, less punk, except for one important thing: his radio show was still the primary way kids outside of Hollywood, outside of fashionable circles, and maybe even outside of the radius of an easy Saturday night jaunt to Sunset Boulevard, heard the latest local and international punk. He brought punk rock music to the real outsiders—the geeks in the outlying areas who lacked a scene to attach themselves to.

Part of the problem was with the contested nature of the definition of punk. Because becoming a punk was such a personal decision, involving one's opinion of oneself, as well as of the world, the punk scene would inevitably be fragmented. And as alienation was one of the main reasons for becoming a punk, there was no reason to believe that some would not be alienated within the scene, especially given its often cliquish or elitist nature. Further, the newer punks were increasingly younger than most of the early punks had been. Many of them were adolescents who encountered punk for the first time not hanging out on the streets of Hollywood or in the clubs, but by listening to "Rodney on the ROQ," reading through the back pages of *Creem*, or watching some media exposé. This younger crowd, however, saw punk as a way to discover, or even create, who they were. The establishment of identity through punk took on greater significance for them than it had for the earlier punks who had come to it in their twenties.

While Shaw's plea for tolerance and inclusiveness may have made sense in terms of creating a vital artistic scene around rock 'n' roll, punk could no longer be maintained within artistic definitions. And while early L.A. punks had been motivated by boredom, "art damage," and their antipathy toward the music business, the newer punk rockers were inspired by new types of boredom and antipathy, born out of and directed at everyday life in postsuburbia. Not only did these new kids feel welcomed by punk rock, but they felt emboldened to remake it in their own image and to claim the turf as their own. If the whole history of rock 'n' roll was to be destroyed, then it might well need to include early punk rock.

One reason why kids in the outer regions could see themselves becoming punks, without the help of the Hollywood hip, had to do with the geography of the area. If you were in Hollywood, you were not necessarily at the center of things. With the Masque more often closed than open, and the Whisky and Starwood seemingly changing their booking policies every month, there were no steady venues for punk rock in the Hollywood area. Occasional shows were held at the Larchmont Hall, on the edges of Hollywood, but early on punks were going anywhere they could to find places to play, from the San Fernando Valley to Orange County. And with major labels uninterested in L.A. punk, the Hollywood scene developed little national reputation or fame to attract others who would reproduce the scene in a faithful fashion. The kids outside of Hollywood could buy the Ramones and Sex Pistols albums and make of it what they would. And they did.

The Masque survived long enough to instantly become legendary as the place for L.A. punk. But once it was gone, there was no center to the scene as far as performing was concerned, so punks went wherever they could. Thus no person, or idea, or locale could claim exclusive ownership. Undoubtedly the Masque was king; the Canterbury was where the in-the-know outcasts lived and practiced. But they all had to travel all over the vast sprawl of the L.A. basin in search of venues to perform—to Hollywood, to downtown, to the Valley, to Arcadia, even to Camarillo State Mental Hospital.[30] Something similar had happened in London where venues were difficult to find because of punk's notoriety. In L.A., however, the problem was more one of infrastructure; there were not that many clubs available to bands that performed original material, and those that did exist were more tied in with the L.A. studio system and the country rock exemplified by the Eagles, Linda Ronstadt, et al. Outside the arenas, live rock 'n' roll in L.A. was hard to come by from 1977 to 1978.

And when punks were invited to perform at a traditional venue, such as the Troubadour, a famous folk club, being punks, they dutifully trashed the place.[31]

There was a flurry of DIY vinyl production during this period. The L.A. punk revolt attacked the music business not because it was "capitalist," but because it put out shit. Some punks may have seen that as the inevitable result of corporate capitalism, but for most the solution was not a political and economic revolution, but a cultural one: make your own noise, "make the music go bang!" as John Doe and Exene Cervenka of X screamed. If there was nowhere established to make your noise, then make your own space to gather and make noise. And if there was no one willing to write about your noise, then make your own magazine to write about your noise. From the beginning, however, there was a certain faith that what they were doing was so brilliant the men in suits wouldn't be able to ignore it forever. Much as rock 'n' roll in the 1950s had forced the music business to pay attention, punk would awaken the dormant biz.[32] And just as a new generation raised on rock 'n' roll eventually took over the business, so, some punks thought, would a new generation supplant the long-haired, coke-snorting, hot-tubbing, pseudo-hippie corporate rock executives who had inherited positions of power in the 1970s. L.A. punks, situated as they were at the center of the international pop culture factory complex, saw themselves as the necessary and inevitable heirs. The do-it-yourself ethic of punk took hold in L.A. because there was no other way to get it done; those who had the money and power to get it done were fucking up so badly.

The result was sometimes suggestive of the stance of an outsider waiting to get in—a stance which increased the ambiguity and tension in the punk scene. So, for example, when Hollywood called, in the form of an invitation to the Dickies to appear on a New Wave-themed episode of the Don Rickles sitcom *C.P.O. Sharkey*, L.A. punks were uncertain how to react. Certainly, there was something perversely perfect about the fit between Rickles, the king of insult comedy, and the Dickies, the current rage on the L.A. scene, as punks pogoed furiously at their shows to their rapid-fire, over-the-top, showbiz assault on such joke-punk songs as "You Drive Me Ape (You Big Gorilla)." L.A. punks mixed feelings of pride and glee with fear and anger. One punk remarked in *Slash*, "Hopefully, the promo and the dough will outweigh the ludicrous rip-off of a script that

The Dickies on *C.P.O. Sharkey,* March 1978.
© Jenny Lens Punk Archive/Cache Agency.

makes everything you all think of 'New Wave' is about one sick, cringing, shotgunned joke."[33] Punks began to whisper that maybe the Dickies were only exploiting the scene.

The tension over whether punk's expansion represented success or failure came to a head in L.A. in 1979. While much of the exciting and exceptional music was being recorded in studios and performed weekly at the reopened Masque, the Whisky a Go-Go, the Starwood, Madame Wongs, and any other club that would have it, the original punk scene lost its cohesiveness. Maybe it was the Sex Pistols' show that kicked off that process, or maybe it was the closing of the Masque. Maybe it was the Masque benefit at the Elks Lodge. Maybe it was dissension within the scene, or the nature of the often nihilist punk ideology. The scene at the Canterbury quickly disintegrated as punks came in conflict with other tenants, and the complex was boarded up on January 14, 1979.[34] The New Masque opened at another locale in Hollywood about the same time, but did not last through the year. And by the summer of 1979, heroin infiltrated the Hollywood scene.[35]

Still, ever growing numbers of kids from the outer regions flocked to the gigs. At the same time as the kids were discovering punk rock, so were the critics and the A&R men.

"Anybody wanna fight?"

By 1979 the British charts were taken over by New Wave. In June of that year, Graham Parker appeared at the Starwood. The British rocker was one of the leading acts among the imported New Wavers who had emerged in the wake of punk. In England, Parker, Elvis Costello, Nick Lowe, Joe Jackson, the Boomtown Rats, and others had taken punk's sneering rebel stance and mixed it with a more accessible, poppier sound. Whereas in England New Wave constituted a genre of its own, with some of the best postpunk music being produced by the likes of Costello and Lowe, in the United States the label became simply a sales category.

The distinction between punk and New Wave went beyond the music. As more and more people came out to see the new music performed live, the insiders lost control over the scene, and thus of the meaning of punk. Subcultural capital could be retained by demonstrating one's devotion, and one way to prove that was to show that one had been on the scene since the beginning. But that could not necessarily be demonstrated on a moment's notice, by style or attitude. A more successful way to show commitment was by dressing punk, in ways that the faint of heart and less devout would not. A year or two earlier, almost any strange dress and strange noise could qualify as punk or New Wave, but now more precise labels were needed. The labels helped to define a subculture, but they were also useful for descriptive purposes: punk meant hard. Over the next few years, the musical borders shattered as all sorts of new and old music was crafted and recombined by bands in clubs all over the area, and the need for differentiation increased.

Punks began to reject the New Wave label because unlike power pop, for instance, the label was insufficiently descriptive of a musical genre. By 1979 or 1980, New Wave was no more than a commercial proposition.

The uniform became codified—straight leg pants, skinny tie, striped shirt, space-age sunglasses. "Fuck the New Wave!" a *Slash* writer fulminated in April 1980. "That's right. It has (not so) suddenly become necessary to draw the line. . . . Something has gone drastically wrong and they won't get away with it. They have o so conveniently just decided that you and I are simply part of something perfectly legitimate. . . . We ain't it, we don't buy it, we don't believe it, we don't identify with it, we don't dance to it and we don't like you."[36] Whereas earlier the struggle had been an internal one, now the enemy was "they," record company executives in ponytails and spandex, "parasitic scum" fishing for the next big thing. L.A. punks had always hated the music business for its complacency, ignorance, and bad taste. Now they felt that their scene was being invaded.

New wave was looking more and more like the next big thing. The economic downturn of 1979 saw gross music sales drop for the first time in the decade, so the industry was desperate to discover something new.[37] In Los Angeles, the physical center of the pop record business, there was a musical renaissance, with clubs sprouting all over to cater to the growing audience for new music. The increase in live venues signaled a musical revival growing out of the punk/New Wave scene. On the heels of the chart success of New Wave in England, and the mild success of New Yorkers Blondie and Patti Smith, record company executives began to scout the L.A. clubs looking for bands to sign.

Then the Knack hit it big. The "ultimate 'skinny tie' band," producing sugarcoated power pop, topped the charts in 1979 with their debut album *Get the Knack* and single "My Sharona."[38] The major labels descended, signing thirty local bands in the next year and a half. The *Los Angeles Times* highlighted the local scene, no longer deferring to New York or resting solely on the achievements of the Laurel Canyon country-folk rockers.[39] Even Doug Weston, whose Troubadour had previously been trashed by punks, wanted in on the action and began booking some of the safer New Wave acts. While older punk bands like X, the Alley Cats, and the Plugz received mild interest from the industry, most of the attention was aimed at power-poppers like 20/20, the Quick, and the Plimsouls. Not all of these bands were awful, and not all were jumping on the bandwagon. The Motels, signed to A&M Records, had been slogging it out for longer than any of the punk bands on the scene. But after the success of the Knack, the record companies were looking for immediate returns on

The Go-Gos performing in 1980.
© Jenny Lens Punk Archive/Cache Agency.

their investments, and only one of the L.A. bands signed at the time—the Go-Gos, with their poppy, girl-group sound—managed to make anything like a career in the majors. The rest of the bands were unceremoniously dumped, each in their turn, as they failed at being "the next big thing."

On the same night as Graham Parker was playing the Starwood, the English punk band The Damned returned to L.A. for a couple of shows at the Whisky. They played their typical theatrical, scrambling, thrashing set, as Dave Vanian, dressed in white face makeup and a Dracula cape, lurched around the stage and climbed the rafters. At the end of their first set of the night, Rat Scabies came out from behind his drum kit to taunt the L.A. punk aesthetes. "Anybody wanna fight?!" he shouted from the stage in his cockney snarl to the Hollywood Day-Glo set assembled below. Up onto the stage leapt a kid with a buzzed head dressed in a flannel shirt, combat fatigues, and army boots. The kid looked like no other punk in the place—no more than fifteen years old, he was easily the youngest person in the club. The kid was from Hermosa Beach, an hour and a half away from the Whisky a Go-Go. Rat Scabies gave the troublemaker a sound thrashing before the bouncers intervened to eject him. With the help of The Damned's manager, however, the young punk soon sneaked in through the back door, and when the second set began, he was right back on the "dance floor."

To conclude the second set, Rat Scabies hit someone else in the audience over the head with a guitar.[40] Another transformation within punk was being signaled, a change fostered by the particular landscape of post-suburban Southern California.

Hardcore Punk, Consumerism, and the Family

Penelope Spheeris's documentary *The Decline of Western Civilization*, filmed between December 1979 and May 1980, caught the Southern California punk scene at a transitional moment. Interviews and live footage from older Hollywood-based punk bands like X, the Bags, and the Germs were mixed with the postsuburban bands Black Flag and the Circle Jerks. Many of the people in the film, at least those filmed in the pit area immediately in front of the stage, were the newer, buzz-headed hardcore punks skanking or slam-dancing—what one bouncer from the Whisky called "a cross between a wild Lindy Hop and the Roller Derby."[1] The film made no mention of the fragmentation within the scene, but the cover of the soundtrack album would prove prophetic.

The cover photo shows Darby Crash, lead singer of the Germs, lying face up on the stage, looking dead. Makeup on his face drips like blood as his hand clutches a microphone. An iron cross dangles from a locked chain around his neck. Darby Crash—known earlier as Bobby Pyn—was one of the original Hollywood punks who went on to become the biggest "star" on the scene, with an almost hypnotic control over his fans and followers. As one punk remembered, "He was a cult leader in every sense of the word," with a "bizarre magnetic power" over people.[2] His signature

Darby Crash (formerly Bobby Pyn, formerly Jan Paul Beahm) at the Masque, November 1977.
© Jenny Lens Punk Archive/Cache Agency.

line, "Hey, gimme a beer," was most often complied with, and followers burned cigarettes into their own and others' arms—the "Germs burn." He was the archetype of the L.A. punk, the most influential singer for the new breed of hardcore punk, and already a local legend.[3]

In the summer of 1980, Darby took off for England where punk, after a passé period, was being revitalized by bands such as Crass. Checking out the scene, he ended up hanging out with Adam Ant, the latest project of former Sex Pistols manager Malcolm McLaren. When Darby returned to L.A., he had added feathers and a mohawk haircut to his leather and chains. This adaptation of London's current "antmusic" fad wardrobe to the local hardcore look spawned a sweeping readjustment of the local punk fashion.

The Germs.
Courtesy of Ronn Spencer.

Even though Darby was still influential to the younger and newer punks, and despite the success of a Germs reunion show, he and his music were left behind as punk became even louder, harder, tougher than the Germs' sound. When the Germs broke up, he put together the Darby Crash Band, but managed to play only one show at the Starwood. Because he had talked about killing himself for so many years, nobody believed him when he threatened to do it after the show. On December 7, 1980, Darby overdosed on heroin. He was found lying under a handwritten sign on the wall proclaiming, "Here lies Darby Crash," with an arrow pointing down.

Punk, as it originally emerged in New York and London, had been identified with both the working class and the avant-garde. Even if it is difficult to support the contention that the original punks were uniformly working class, certainly the rhetoric and style of much of punk—from the

Ramones' blue-jeans-and-leather-jacket look to the Clash's anticapitalist ragings—positioned the genre as, in part, an attack on bourgeois complacency and government control. Even Los Angeles produced some working-class punk, most notably the Dils who briefly embraced the hammer and sickle logo of international communism in singing "I Hate the Rich" and calling for a "Class War." The other original thread in punk came from the avant-garde tradition, whether it was New Yorker Patti Smith's echoes of American beatniks or the Sex Pistols' use of the Situationist-inspired artwork of Jamie Reid. Bands such as the Talking Heads and X-Ray Spex were stocked with art-school students, graduates, and dropouts. In early L.A. punk, two sources of talent were the Venice Beach poetry scene and the local performance-art scene.

Early critics and scholars of punk attempted to define punk in terms of its relationship to contemporary social relations. Was punk an expression of working-class youth revolt or an avant-garde artistic movement giving voice to a wide-ranging critique in the spirit of the Dadaists of the early twentieth century? The first important study of punk rock, and one of the groundbreaking works of cultural studies, was Dick Hebdige's *Subculture: The Meaning of Style* (1979). Building on the work on British postwar youth cultures pioneered by the Birmingham School and synthesizing numerous strands of poststructuralist theory, Hebdige located British punk in the tradition of youth "revolt through style." Punk was a self-contained, working-class, youth subculture that used style to communicate its message of alienation and discontent. Punk, according to Hebdige, directly reflected the conditions of white, working-class youth in 1970s England as a subculture that expressed "a fundamental tension between those in power and those condemned to subordinate positions and second-class lives."[4] Punk expressed, through style and noise, the real-life situations of working-class kids living on the dole in a declining welfare state and fallen British empire.

Simon Frith added an important corrective to Hebdige's claim that the punk subculture presented "an oblique challenge to hegemony." In *Sound Effects: Youth, Leisure, and the Politics of Rock 'n' roll* (1981), Frith rejected the interpretation of punk as a reflection of lived experience, seeing the first punks as "a self-conscious, artful lot" responding to both "rock tradition and populist cliché; their music no more reflected directly back on conditions in the dole queue than it emerged spontaneously from them."[5]

According to Frith, one of the traditions, one of the dialogues, in which the scholar must situate punk was the history of rock 'n' roll and its particular tradition of blending art and commerce. Frith argued that punk was responding to music itself, not reflecting the lives of working-class youth.

Certainly, early L.A. punk was no working-class revolt. But, as bad as punks perceived the music business to be, theirs was not solely a response to stagnation in that world. L.A. punk responded equally to the city around it. And that city, unlike London or New York, was no traditional city.

Postsuburban Southern California

Los Angeles has always seemed different. The "fragmented metropolis," the "suburban metropolis," the "decentralized city," it offers a distinct contrast to the traditional eastern city, which is characterized by a definite urban core.[6] In fact, Los Angeles has been "at the forefront of new urbanization trends" since the late nineteenth century.[7]

Los Angeles began its spectacular growth in the 1880s, when the Southern Pacific Railroad linked the region to the rest of the country and artesian well technology transformed the scruffy, arid plains and foothills into fertile, irrigated fields.[8] The combined forces of land speculation and streetcar development led to the notorious sprawl of the L.A. metro area in the years around the turn of the century, as the Pacific Electric Railway Company joined "streetcar suburbs" west to east from Santa Monica to San Bernardino and north to south from Pasadena to Balboa.[9]

Even before the 1920s, when the automobile became the major mode of transportation, Los Angeles developed in opposition to the eastern urban model of concentration, with "transportation, water, and real estate" contributing to the city's extraordinary rate of growth in both size and population.[10] Because land was widely available for development and the real estate industry was largely unregulated, "thousands of subdividers converted rural acreage into suburban lots from San Fernando to Long Beach, Santa Monica to Sierra Madre."[11] In the first quarter of the century, affluent suburban developments stretched west of downtown into Beverly Hills, Holmby Hills, Westwood, Bel Air, Brentwood, and Pacific Palisades; eastward along the foothills of the San Gabriel Mountains to Pasadena,

San Marino, and Arcadia; and southward along the coast in Palos Verdes. Discoveries of oil all over the area in the 1890s and again in the 1920s gave rise to scores of working-class suburbs throughout the area, especially in eastern and southern Los Angeles County and northern Orange County.[12]

Thus was born the diversity of land uses and settlement patterns that the word "suburbia" fails to fully capture. The "black gold suburbs" differed in nearly every way from the middle-class housing developments that sprouted in the San Fernando Valley after its annexation by Los Angeles in 1915, and from the upper middle-class suburbs of Beverly Hills, Palos Verdes, and Pasadena.[13] But common to all was the dominance of the single-family, detached house. By 1930, "about 94 percent of all dwellings in Los Angeles were single-family houses, a figure unmatched by any other city."[14]

The widespread availability of cheap land, the oil fields and refineries scattered around the region, the largest mass transit system in the world, and the preference for detached houses provided the basis for the amorphous sprawl of Los Angeles in the first decades of the twentieth century. That sprawl grew in the 1920s when the proponents of a vast system of road building won out over those who wanted to expand the interurban rail system. The Pacific Electric Company declined and then collapsed as local governments paid for new roads and developers bought up and subdivided land along the new and incredibly ambitious system of major north-south and east-west boulevards. By the end of the twenties, Los Angeles was already a "decentralized city," with industry and shopping facilities spread throughout the area instead of concentrated in the downtown core, and auto traffic criss-crossing in every direction.[15]

In the thirties and forties, the Automobile Club of Southern California produced a master plan for expanding the network of roads, linking the whole area by more than five hundred miles of limited-access freeways. Throughout this period, the movie industry, which had begun to relocate to the area in the teens, broadcast the image of the Southern California way of life across the country, encouraging a steady stream of migration to the region. World War II added the aircraft industry to the oil and movie industries as major employers in the area, attracting millions of dollars, jobseekers, home buyers, and commuters. The area continued to grow in the same way after the war, fostered by the region-wide system of freeways first proposed by business leaders in 1942, and underwritten by the Interstate Highway Act of 1956. First the San Fernando Valley and then the San Gabriel Valley to the east and the South Bay region and northern Orange County to the south began to sprout huge residential subdivisions on recently rural soil.[16]

The trend was national. Through a mixture of economic, demographic, and political transformations, suburbia became "postsuburbia." In Nassau and Suffolk counties on Long Island, along the Route 128 corridor outside Boston, in Silicon Valley in northern California, in the Houston, Texas, area, and, especially, in the Los Angeles and Orange County region of Southern California, bedroom communities grew into "edge cities": self-sufficient, mixed-use regions of housing, factories, offices, shops, and services.[17] Just as the U.S. census of 1890 declared the western frontier closed, the census of 1970 declared the closing of another frontier: the "crabgrass frontier."[18] By 1970 more people in the United States lived in suburbs than in cities or rural areas, but the nature of suburbia itself was dramatically different.[19] While the reality of suburban life was always more complex than the popular image of "ticky-tacky houses" on "cookie-cutter lots," by the moment of suburbia's seeming ascendance in the 1970s, it had already changed from its traditional form as a homogeneous, residential community on the outer edge of an older urban area.[20]

Postwar development and suburban growth exacerbated the decentralized nature of L.A., with dramatic social consequences, particularly in terms of racial segregation. In historian Kenneth Jackson's view, "There were two necessary conditions for American residential deconcentration—the suburban ideal and population growth—and two fundamental causes—racial prejudice and cheap housing."[21] Nowhere was this more true than in Los Angeles. The city differed from eastern cities in that most of the ghettoes that developed were not in public housing complexes but in the original single-family bungalow communities of the streetcar era, long since abandoned by both the railway and white residents. But while the low-density housing might have seemed to represent the suburban ideal, the Watts rebellion of 1965 showed that racial segregation in housing reflected and reinforced inequalities in power.[22] Soon there was a proliferation of incorporated municipalities with separate, and often separatist, governmental units.[23] White, middle-class citizens in many of these outer municipalities sought, and discovered, ways to avoid the burdens of citizenship (read: taxes), while shifting the costs of social services to the poor and people of color still living within the confines of L.A. proper.

If the rise of the American city (and the accompanying rise of the intertwined ideals of youth culture and mass culture) can be seen as a particular historical development, tied to the emergence of industrial capitalism in the late nineteenth century, the emergence of postsuburbia was also part of a larger transformation in the history of capitalism, as the spatial expression of the stage of advanced capitalism. People increasingly moved into the suburbs after World War II not only because they saw them as a "bourgeois utopia," but also because that was where the jobs were. And the jobs were there not only because of cheap land and government policies promoting freeway construction, but also because of new industries that needed new factories and offices, and the expanding service and retail sectors that followed residents.[24] In addition, the oil embargo of 1973 accelerated the shift away from the Fordist model of production. With the country bogged down in a "deep fiscal and legitimation crisis," companies "found themselves with a lot of unusable excess capacity (chiefly idle plants and equipment) under conditions of intensifying competition."[25] Flexibility and mobility with respect to labor, markets, and products became key to corporate success. At the same time, declining transportation costs and expanding satellite communications technologies made the location of the office, factory, or sales outlet less important to capital. The growing number of high-tech aerospace, communications, electronics, and computer industries and the new service, information, and consulting industries in medical technology, software, and energy did not require a centralized, urban location.[26] With the arrival of the computer age, work could even be done from home.

From "Art-damaged" to "Damaged"

Down the coast from Hollywood, in Hermosa Beach and Huntington Beach, punk was reborn with a new face, ready to fight at a moment's notice. Postsuburban punk arose both in descent from and in opposition to local musical developments and in response to local social and political conditions. From the very beginning of the Hollywood scene, punks had come in from all over the area, yet had tried to identify themselves as part of the scene. But even then there were some who preferred to maintain outsider status, coming in to Hollywood for the shows, then retreating to their homes in the exurbs. The zine *Flipside* was started by five recent Whittier High School graduates in May 1977, hitting the streets just weeks after *Slash*'s debut. One hundred copies of a twenty-page xerox zine sold at shows for a quarter each. Pooch, one of the founders, remembered that they liked to return to Whittier, twenty-five miles inland, after the shows and make fun of the Hollywood punks.[27] And as early as 1978, a couple of singles were recorded, produced, and distributed by exurban punks on homegrown record labels. Hermosa's Black Flag released their seven-inch EP "Nervous Breakdown" on their own SST label in the middle of the year; it was followed by "Out of Vogue" by Santa Ana and Fullerton's Middle Class on Billy Star's Joke Records. The different experiences of these two bands are instructive about what was happening to the punk scene. There was a new taxonomy of tastes within punk rock, and the new attitudes and aesthetics all ultimately rejected the urban hipsterism of the Hollywood scene.

The Middle Class—three brothers (ages fifteen, seventeen, and twenty-one) and a friend from Santa Ana and Fullerton down in Orange County—had ventured the two-hour drive into the Hollywood scene as early as 1978, when they went to Brendan Mullen hoping for a gig at the Masque and almost got laughed at all the way home. "Having been advised to cut their hair and punk-out their dress, they were summarily dismissed to the suburbs, presumably to pass into a well-deserved obscurity," one zine writer observed. "However, fate intervened in the form of Hector of the Zeros who booked them as opening support for a show featuring the Controllers and the Germs and, after that, for the next six months, they played support to many of the local Hollywood scene bands."[28] After their first show at Larchmont Hall in April, where the crowd "stood in a semicircle and nobody moved," they gigged regularly as the token "suburban" band.[29] *Slash* referred to their first show in a column titled "The 'Hey, You Mean They Got Punks in Those Places??' Dept." Noting the blasé reaction and blank stares the Middle Class received, *Slash* commented, "sometimes them scene-making punx are worse than the fuckin' Spanish Inquisition!" and asked the prescient question, "Will the next New Wave come from the great Wasteland?"[30] (This at a time when the term "new wave" had not yet been rejected.)

The Hollywood scene accepted the Middle Class, at least to some extent.

The Controllers.
Courtesy of Ronn Spencer.

But even when some of their members moved into the Canterbury, they did not lose their identity as a "suburban" band, and the insider crowd did not quite know what to do with them. Taking the stage looking "like a bunch of rampaging Scientologists," they defied all fashion and music conventions even at a moment when conventions were not so rigidly set within punk. By the summer of 1978, they were making converts, as this *Slash* review attests: "These guys looked normal. Like high school normal. Like chemistry class normal. Like writing a paper in the library normal. How come they sounded like twisted metal air raids and dynamite fumes? I was shocked. If you look like that, you're not supposed to sound like that. Yet it was obvious: the mob was pogoing with genuine furor, the aggression meter was in the red zone, this was certified punk fever grade triple-A beware of imitations. I've seen fast bands but these unknowns run with the best." The reviewer concluded, "And that curly-haired singer should, according to the basic laws of physics, end up with his vocal chords tied in a knot after 5 minutes."[31] Another *Slash* reviewer the following month described their shows as "intense, teeth-gritting affairs that leave the participant dazed, stunned, even irritated." The reviewer noted the "chaos and confusion" that resulted from "the incitable nature of their strange, assaulting music coupled with the growing number of their unpredictably rabid fans." The cumulative effect was "not unlike kissing a semi at full speed."[32]

The Middle Class never brought their own crowd of fans and followers with them to Hollywood, but they never completely left their post-suburban home, either. Like traditional bohemians, and like other L.A. punks, they made the trip into the city to enact their art. But they did not reinvent themselves completely in the process. They didn't change their names, and they didn't change their dress. The cover of "Out of Vogue"—a diatribe against mass culture—depicts a mundane Southern California suburban scene: two young girls stand in the middle of a street, surrounded and almost dwarfed by the still life of a housing tract with Big Wheels, a basketball backboard, and a Volkswagen bus in a driveway. The cover scene portrayed not only their roots, but their continuing daily reality as "the Middle Class," and they returned to these images throughout their career.[33] As a postsuburban band, the Middle Class redefined the aesthetics of punk, both musically and visually.

A similar aesthetic shift occurred at the same time in Hermosa Beach with the formation of Black Flag. Their long-time engineer, Spot, captured the band's early sound and fury in describing his brief stint as their bass player:

> Greg invited me to play bass with them and I accepted. Sure, it's something to do. The band rehearsed deep within the bowels of the Hermosa Bath House. So one night I walked down to the Strand, banged on the door and went in. Greg gave me this funky cheapo bass guitar and I plugged it in. He picked up his guitar and started playing loud distorted atonal riffs and I cringed and wondered what I was doing in this dank decrepit dungeon with these strange cretins. The band had a total of six songs, each of which lasted no more than one minute. Greg showed me the simple repetitive chords—"Ok, do you want to try it?"
>
> Sure, why not. Ok, here we go. 1-2-3-4!! and BANG!! the drummer started smashing out a fast trashy straight 4 pattern and the wiry little

singer started bellowing and jumping around wildly and Greg's body lurched forward as he underwent a remarkable transition from Jeckyl to Hyde. His head shook, eyes flashed and teeth bared maniacally as he began to grind thick chords out of a guitar that in the shadowy light could have been mistaken for a chainsaw. Within seconds it was over. Jeckyl calmly stepped out of his Hyde as if stepping out of a routine nightmare.

"You want to try it again?" "Uh, uh, uh, uh, uh, well uh, yeah. . . ." I was dumbfounded, shocked, my eyes wide in amazement, my mouth hanging open in disbelief. We played again. 1-2-3-4!! Jeckyl became Hyde. Music became Noise. Punk rock became a resident of Hermosa Beach.

Ten minutes later we had played the entire six song set twice.[34]

As punk rock was musically reborn in the communities outside of Los Angeles, it challenged the subcultural boundaries as well. As much by design as by accident, Black Flag never became a part of the Hollywood scene. They remained in Hermosa Beach, where they moved into "the Church," an actual old church that had been converted into rehearsal and living space. The band felt ostracized from the Hollywood scene. "We couldn't get gigs," Greg Ginn complained, "because we were from outside of the established scene. We just rehearsed for two years." Chuck Dukowski, the bass player, added: "In Hollywood, everybody's in the middle of the city, and if you're not from Hollywood, you're not a city person, and you're not urban, you're not tough, you're not a punk. They look at us, we dress like we do, we're from the beach area, and they just kinda go, 'SURE you want a gig. Right. Fuck off.'"[35] They didn't even record in Hollywood. Despite talk of making a record for Chris D.'s Upsetter label or Greg Shaw's Bomp Records, ultimately they had to produce and distribute their own vinyl, starting SST Records in the process.

Black Flag cultivated the outsider stance, rejecting what they saw as "the overly-glittered rock 'n' roll world of Hollywood."[36] As the original lead singer, Keith Morris, claimed when asked why they didn't just move to Hollywood, "We hate Hollywood! That's the big scene out there. Fuck that scene." Another punk chimed in, "90% of punk-rockers in L.A. are just old Bowie freaks."[37] Punk rock was being redefined as antiurban, antidecadence, anti-art—as hardcore. *Flipside* compared the scene at the Church to the earlier days of the Masque, calling the Church "more underground" and claiming, "The kids that live here are also very different than the early Masque crowd, there's no art damage, no rich kid poseurs and no money hungry jerks."[38] Hardcore punk took root as the antidote to new wave posing, emphasizing punk rock purity. Art-damaged was replaced by just plain *Damaged*—the title of Black Flag's first album.

Even farther down the coast, another scene was developing around a few bands from Long Beach and Huntington Beach. Rhino 39, out of Millikan High School in Long Beach, began making the trip up to Hollywood in 1978. In Huntington Beach (or "Aitch-Bee," as it was called) the Crowd (from Edison High), the Klan, Vicious Circle, the Skrews, the Slashers, and the Outsiders played backyard parties. Most of the bands were made up of high school kids who stopped being jocks, hippies, surfers, or whatever, and instead became punks. In late 1978 and early 1979, such transformations were made all down the coast, first by a few, then by more and more.

New punk bands emerged in droves, and while many of them merely played the 1-2-3-4 sound of the Ramones as fast as they could, others introduced interesting variations, combining diverse influences and sounds. Over the next couple of years bands from around the South Bay and inland Orange County came to play parties in Huntington Beach—new bands like the Circle Jerks, Red Cross, the Adolescents, Agent Orange, and Social Distortion, in addition to the Middle Class and Black Flag. Eventually a couple of key clubs began to book hardcore punk shows in postsuburbia: the Cuckoo's Nest in Costa Mesa and the Fleetwood in Redondo Beach. Several factions emerged within the scene south of L.A., including the Day-Glo surf set, the leather and chains crowd, and the inland punks. By 1980, residential communities all over the southland were home to at least a punk or two. The punks were scattered geographically but united by the fact that they stayed in their postsuburban towns—many because they still lived at home, attending high school or junior high. Even those who seemingly had nothing to keep them there—runaways and "grown-ups"—stayed and developed punk rock scenes. Eddie of Eddie and the Subtitles described Orange County as "an unbelievable, mindless, sexless, funless monster that should be permanently shut down," but he continued to live there, performing and recording with his own bands, producing and managing others, and fostering a scene in the Fullerton–Anaheim area.[39]

The aesthetics of the new hardcore punk were defined less by the sound of the music—much of which was Ramones-derived and Germs-inspired, with a hint of sixties beach rock—and more by the style of dress and behavior. The main musical innovation was to make punk rock faster and noisier if possible—in a word, worse. "There has always been a surplus of lousy 'rock' bands," said punk writer Joe Carducci, "but hardcore was perhaps the first time on the planet that there was a fad for them."[40] There *was* musical innovation, experimentation, even sounds that expanded rock 'n' roll's horizons. Black Flag's Greg Ginn was listed as one of the ten most influential guitarists of the 1980s by *Musician* magazine, while the undeniable influence of bands like the Adolescents and the Descendents can be heard in contemporary punk artists such as Blink 182 and Green Day. But the DIY ethos combined with the hardcore punk aesthetic to produce some barely listenable "music." First of all, DIY meant that musical talent and proficiency were not required. And the way most punk shows were structured, with five or more bands sharing the bill, opening slots were often reserved for new bands that were just learning their chops.

Hardcore emphasized punk's exclusivity, and a valuable way to keep out the uncommitted was to make music that only the committed could tolerate or appreciate. This became especially important after the emergence of new wave as the commercial alternative to punk, and after MTV launched in 1980 with its stable of new wave performers. Hardcore punks aimed their most vicious assaults at the new wave "poseurs," those who thought punk was a fun way to dress up on a Saturday night. It took well-trained ears to distinguish between the sounds of Modern Warfare and RF7, or even between the individual songs of any given band. And it took true commitment to suffer through a half dozen or more such soundalike bands in a row—especially when fights were breaking out all around you.

Hollywood punks began to notice the transformation from punk to hardcore in 1979, with a mixture of reactions. When the Buzzcocks, a British punk band, came to town, the beach punks made their presence known, storming the stage, dancing the H.B. strut—elbows high, arms and legs flailing, moving backward into other punks—and diving into the audience. The show was held at the Santa Monica Civic Auditorium, a decidedly nonpunk venue that held several thousand people, signaling punk's burgeoning popularity.

The postsuburban punks claimed the scene as theirs through their behavior, drawing lines of distinction not only around the sound of the music, but also in terms of proper punk conduct. The security guards, having never seen this type of behavior, started throwing punks off the stage, only to see waves of others climbing up to take their place. The *Times'* Richard Cromelin complained about the disruptions and the irresponsible behavior of the fans, but the *Slash* reviewers embraced the "kids" for invigorating what was otherwise a rather dull performance. And at one point during the set, a "bleached blond spikey pinhead" reached the stage, skanked across, and shouted "Huntington Beach!" into the microphone before being muscled back into the crowd by the security forces. Finally, the Buzzcocks' singer invited the kids to sit up on the stage, and hundreds gathered around the band as they ripped into their songs with a new vehemence. A *Slash* reviewer remarked, "This was the real thing, live and anarchistic."[41]

The beach punks simultaneously revitalized and fragmented punk. By the end of 1980, there were simply too many people into punk in the greater L.A. area for the scene to be contained in a small club like the Masque, split up into a few little snobbish cliques. As audiences became larger, they also became more divided. Musical styles proliferated, all under the rubric of "punk." New zines emerged, including *We Got Power* (Santa Monica), *Outcry* (South Pasadena), and *Rag in Chains* (Hollywood), which was edited by a thirteen-year-old who called himself Shreader. Scenes sprouted in outlying areas like Fullerton and the San Fernando Valley, and eventually from San Diego to Santa Barbara. Within a couple of years, one writer could hyperbolically claim in the liner notes to a Southern California compilation album that hardcore punk was "digging its way into every suburban high school in the U.S. . . . Today's Hardcore is the most dominant, the most obvious scene in the American music underground."[42]

By this point, the Hollywood scene had lost its dominance in the L.A. area. Some older punks embraced the change as refreshing. Many had burned out after being in the scene for two or three years. Others sank into heroin addiction. Many older punks could not be bothered to make the journey down to places like Costa Mesa and Redondo Beach to see bands—especially since they would be greeted upon arrival with jeers and fists for being too old and "new wave." Others continued to make music, even gaining a degree of mainstream respectability (the kiss of death for hardcore authenticity); X, for example, was named the band of the year in 1980 by the *Times* in honor of their debut album *Los Angeles* on Slash Records. The Masque, in its second locale, finally closed for good late in 1979. *Slash*, whose editor, Kickboy Face, attempted to embrace and support the new breed of punks, did not survive the transition from punk to hardcore, publishing its final issue in the summer of 1980. The Masque's Brendan Mullen came out with a new zine, *Slush*, mixing the older punk with the new hardcore, but couldn't get the financing to maintain it beyond a couple of issues.

While the Hollywood punk scene continued to produce bands, zines, and clubs, hardcore had emerged to restore punk to its "purity" in explicit disavowal of new wave, and in a confused combination of reverence for and rejection of art-damaged punk. What is remarkable is that young people in postsuburbia saw within punk rock (which was until then a field ruled by working class and avant-garde sensibilities) the possibility to express themselves and their own social experience. They acted as agents to contest and shape the rules of the subfield of punk rock to their needs. Hardcore punk rock developed in a semiautonomous manner, according to conflicts and contestations within the field of rock 'n' roll and the subfield of punk. But hardcore punk emerged also within the social contexts of postsuburbia and the position of youth in 1970s society.

"No future": Coming of Age in Postsuburbia

Young people coming of age in the 1970s were no longer sure about the state of the world or their own place in it. Sociological studies show that "normal" adolescents now felt "worse about themselves" than had their predecessors from the sixties, who "were more self-confident, controlled, and more trusting of others."[43] Underneath a "superficial harmony" they were feeling "frustration and alienation" and starting to experience "socially produced identity crises."[44] Unlike their counterparts in the sixties, they refused to take part in any kind of social action, feeling no sense of attachment to or ownership of the world around them. In contrast to the idealism and socially oriented thinking of sixties youth, youth in the seventies embraced a radical individualism that was critical of pretty much everything. "From getting up in the morning to trust in government," even "everyday existence" was "difficult to tolerate."[45] In the view of seventies youth, all social institutions lacked legitimacy, and arbitrariness seemed to be the natural order of things

These were now fully "postmodern youth," whose alienation resulted from "the impact of modern information technologies spread by global capitalism," as the corporate-controlled media and consumer environments increasingly supplanted the home, family, school, and workplace as the sites for socialization.[46] Nowhere was this truer than in postsuburbia, where the information technologies and industries had staked their deepest claim. Young people in postsuburbia were now not simply consumers, but "metaconsumers," "both the consumer and the consumed," "not only a consumer of products and symbols but also an active participant in the shopping spectacle." For these young people, "the shopping mall is not merely an economic space where exchanges take place but a symbolic social space for everyone to come alive in" and a "pervasive" metaphor for life.[47] This condition affected youth throughout society, not merely "delinquents" or members of subcultures. All youth—again, especially in postsuburbia—were increasingly hailed, identified, and self-identified as isolated, fragmented, individual consumers, but, unlike previous generations, without the comforts of a generational cohort or a unifying (as a pied piper or as an enemy) mass culture.

Punk rock, originally the music of disaffected bohemians and working-class rebels in cities, was seized by postsuburban youth as an expression of their own boredom. Punk in postsuburbia did not recreate the youth culture revolts of earlier generations, but reflected instead the fragmentation, isolation, and individualism of the 1970s. While earlier punks had wrestled with the leftover ideals of the sixties, hardcore punks rejected them outright. The transition from punk to hardcore, and from the sixties to the eighties, occurred when new punks no longer held out hope for revolution from within or without. The do-it-yourself ethos, for them, provided a retreat from larger social, political, and cultural issues. Greg Shaw and the first L.A. punks aimed much of their attack at the music industry and, only by extension, the ethos of consumerism which the industry supported. Hardcore punks inverted the equation, ignoring the music business and attacking consumerism as a social process, but without any explicit political framework or statement. In this, hardcore punks reflected the social conditions of postsuburbia. As Cameron Crowe discovered when he returned to high school in the 1970s, the "fast times at Ridgemont High" really took place at the mall, the quintessential post-suburban site.[48]

The formation of alternative institutions such as dozens of record labels, zines, clubs, and communal youth organizations can be read as a modernist response to postmodern consumerism and fragmentation, an attempt to create some sense of reality, maybe even authenticity, certainly control over daily life and the future. Through these institutions punks attempted to become producers instead of consumers, combining romantic and individualist ideas with a do-it-yourself anarchism. In this way, the alternative social, economic, and political institutions established by hardcore punks appear as somewhat traditional attempts at production. Punks set up institutions in opposition to the dominant values of consumerism, attempting to create their own semiautonomous public sphere.

When punk rock came along as an available discourse, a significant minority of youth in postsuburbia embraced it as the articulation of dissatisfaction and as a means of overcoming boredom. But still suspicious of any group, they refused to see even punk as a movement. Punks rejected both the dominant culture and anything like a counterculture. They eschewed both community and citizenship, preferring to take refuge in the self, in everyday life. In this hardcore punk resulted from an era of diminished expectations, as both antidote to and reflection of general social ills.

Hardcore Punk and the Family in Postsuburbia

In the 1983 film *Suburbia*, director Penelope Spheeris captures an important aspect of the hardcore punk scene. The kids of the T.R. ("The Rejected") gang, parentless and free, leave the abandoned housing tract they have turned into a squat and drive around in search of criminal mischief to commit. Cruising the empty streets of their former homes— quiet, dimly lit housing tracts and planned communities—they seek out a pristine example of the foundation of suburban comfort: the freshly laid sod of a tract house's front lawn. Without hesitation, and communicating only through giggles, they pile out of their beat-up sedan, roll up the sod, and load it into the trunk. In drunken punk glee, the kids head off to that other symbol of Southern Californian suburban bliss, the mall. Marching through its deserted corridors until they reach the bank of flickering television screens at Radio Shack, they roll out the sod and cuddle up in front of the glowing blue babysitter, as the announcer on the screen discusses how to handle nuclear war as an everyday affair.

Both *Suburbia* and *The Decline of Western Civilization* contributed to a discourse of punk that increasingly problematized images of family and home. In her emphasis on the visual landscape of suburbia, the rejection of punks by their families, and their search for alternative homes, Spheeris echoes the discourse hardcore punks created in songs and zines. The punk kids in *Suburbia* inhabit a house in an abandoned development that is overrun by packs of wild dogs. Their lives revolve around trips in the car from the mall to the strip mall convenience store to the warehouse in the industrial part of town where the punk shows are staged. Despite its title, the film depicts not the clichéd cul-de-sacs and ranch houses or tract homes that the word "suburbia" normally connotes, but the new land-scape of postsuburbia.

Without an urban or political center to serve as a focal point, the heart of postsuburbia was the home. "The true center of this new city," says Robert Fishman, "is not in some downtown business district but in each residential unit. From that central starting point, the members of the household create their own city from the multitude of destinations that are within suitable driving distance."[49] Kenneth Jackson agrees: "Our lives are now centered inside the house, rather than on the neighborhood or the community."[50] Mike Davis has shown how the destruction of public space has made downtown Los Angeles into "Fortress L.A.," and Jackson claims the trend is followed in postsuburbia, which is "returning to the medieval method of building walls and of denying entrance to all but their residents, employees, and visitors."[51] Ironically, the notion of the home as the last remaining hope to fight off the fragmentation of the out-er world came about as the world inside the home was itself fragmenting. Hardcore punk institutions were often designed to counter the fragment-ing effects of consumerist postsuburbia, where the line between home and outside world, between private and public, was blurred.

Spheeris based her fiction film on real punks and real events, and the movie mirrors many punks' experiences. The members of Black Flag started SST Records while they were living in the Church. After being kicked out of there, the band moved around the southern half of Los Angeles County, living for the most part in various places in the South

Bay, and moving the office from Hermosa to Redondo to Torrance to Hollywood, depending on circumstances. Like the earlier Hollywood punks who had lived and partied at the Canterbury Apartments and the Masque, and a few other places like Joan Jett's apartment on San Vicente, or Tomata Du Plenty's allegedly haunted "Wilton Hilton" apartment, hardcore punks attempted to find alternative homes and communities. The Better Youth Organization (BYO) was based in Hollywood's "Skin-head Manor"—"a place where kids from all over Southern California met & exchanged ideas."[52] Created to promote live shows in L.A. and project a better image of punk, BYO was "envisioned as a collective, positive voice . . . as a reaction against police violence, outside exploitation & a general negative outlook held against the Punk/alternative music scene." Mike Ness of the band Social Distortion made his apartment in Fullerton available as a crash pad and party spot, as immortalized in the Social Distortion song "Playpen" as well as in the Adolescents' "Kids of the Black Hole," with the lines,

> Kids in the fast lane
> Living for today
> No rules to abide by
> No one to obey.[53]

The notion of family was deeply ingrained in punk discourse. In "Home Is Where We Hide," the Middle Class sang,

> Families breed inside four walls
> Like they're expected to do
> Uphold standards of living
> Consorts to the myths that they're given.

Milo of the Descendents sang "My Dad Sucks" and "Parents—they're so fucked up / Parents—why don't they shut up" in a wonderfully adenoidal punk-pop whine. Kat of Legal Weapon wrote numerous songs about sexually abusive family situations, concluding, "Daddy's gone mad, and momma's out of her head." Wasted Youth sang about a "Problem Child." The Angry Samoans ranted,

My old man's a fatso
he's got a potbelly for a mouth
My old man's a fatso
but you know he owns this house.

In the 1984 film *Repo Man*, Milo's parents sit like zombies in front of the television watching, and giving all their money to, the television preacher. In *Suburbia*, the parents are divorced, alcoholic, or sexually abusive (leading to a punk girl's suicide). It is tempting see such portrayals as reflections of social reality, to see all punks as the products of broken homes or dysfunctional families. It would be more accurate to see these images as part of the postsuburban hardcore punk discourse. Hardcore extended L.A. punk's antiliberal, anti-California, antihippie stance. At the same time, however, much of this era of punk was aimed at the oppressive, patriarchal nuclear family. Hardcore punk opposed the nuclear family as well as the lack of family structure, protesting against *both* suburban conformity and the disappearance of suburban security.

Ronald Reagan's victory in the 1980 presidential election may have done more than any other event to revitalize punk and ensure its longevity—not only because punks opposed his conservative politics, but because here was an enemy with a face. Whereas earlier Hollywood punk had aimed its critique at hippies (be they music business executives, laid-back California folkies, or liberal politicians), now hardcore punk named Reagan as public enemy number one. The transformation was illustrated most starkly in the song "California Über Alles" by San Francisco's Dead Kennedys. The song was originally an ironic stab at the "zen fascism" of California Governor Jerry Brown, but after Reagan's election, singer Jello Biafra rewrote the lyrics to remove the irony, believing that Reagan's America represented a real threat. While few Southern California bands were as overtly and intellectually political as the Dead Kennedys, Reagan hovered over the scene as the great oppressive father-figure. Lyrics aimed at Reagan, and at the omnipresent specter of World War III, dominated the protest songs of hardcore punk.

Even as Reagan energized punk protest, antipathy toward him redirected and even confused the meaning of punk.[54] Reagan as fascist was an obvious and convenient target, but what about the hippies? Were they still the enemies? With regard to families, the anti-Reagan message made things more confusing, but it also made punk's message more all-encompassing. There was nothing in postsuburbia to embrace as one's own, no matter what type of family one came from. Reagan stood for the Moral Majority's revival of the "traditional family," but the newer, younger punks were the children of baby boomers with more liberal, less traditional notions of child-rearing. The family structure at the time in Orange County was much more emotionally open and less repressive than the traditional suburban, nuclear family. The middle-class family was not isolated from society, as the oedipal family had previously been. The new family was, however, "segmented," rarely gathering together at the same time with "each individual following in part a course separate from the others." While family members were not isolated from society as they had been in suburbia, because kids went to preschool at an early age and the mother worked outside the home, the changes of identity and roles for parent and child were directly connected to the postmodern, postsuburban environment and its exaltation of consumerism.[55] Postsuburban hardcore punk rejected both the traditional and the new types of families—both the Reaganite "fascist" family and the liberal "hippie" family.[56]

Postsuburban punk's addition to, or twist on, the rebellious teen narrative was its particular version of the oedipal tale. While London punk might be seen as a rejection of the mother—the queen presiding over the declining empire or Margaret Thatcher dismantling the welfare state— punk in postsuburban Southern California tried to kill the father. But this father was a confusing figure. Cops everywhere, including those who appeared every week at punk rock gigs, provided a real target for punk rage. They could be seen as fathers with power, black-clad, domineering, inflicting corporal punishment, with Reagan, off in the distance, as the führer of the army of fathers. But Reagan didn't always fit very well in the role of commander, of the father who wielded the belt. He was more like the absent patriarchal father, the one who supposedly ruled with an iron fist in a velvet glove, but who in fact did not rule at all. In punk discourse, the absent patriarchal father vegged out in front of the television, he became gay, he molested his children, he became more and more fascist as he drifted farther and farther from his children, or he disappeared altogether. He was both authoritarian and a cipher, both stupid enough to call punks "punkers" (and this enraged punks), and nasty enough to call out the police and all other forces at his disposal to oppress them.

Possibly the most famous hardcore song of the era, the Suicidal Tendencies' "Institutionalized," tells the story of two parents who put their son in a mental hospital because, in the parents' words, "we're afraid you're gonna hurt somebody / we're afraid you're gonna hurt yourself." The son replies indignantly:

What are you trying to say? *I'm* crazy?
Well I went to *your* schools
I went to *your* churches
I went to *your* institutional learning facilities.
How can you say I'm crazy?

His indignation rises with each line, until he explodes in rage: "All I wanted was a Pepsi, and they wouldn't give it to me/ just one Pepsi . . . and they keep bugging me." The song builds from a grinding opening, with a meandering, metallic guitar lead and spoken lyrics matter-of-factly telling the tale of suburban teen angst, through a series of crescendos, stepping up in speed and intensity, until the chorus is a blinding, raging blur of hardcore punk chords and screaming: "I'm not crazy! You're the one who's crazy! You're driving me crazy!" And then back down again for another spoken verse, to build back up to the chorus. Each verse advances the story of the misunderstood teen and the misunderstanding parents. After the third and final chorus, as the guitars and drums disintegrate, the singer says in resignation, "Doesn't matter, I'll probably get hit by a car anyway." The parents here fulfill both Reagan roles: they take charge, they don't ignore the situation, but then they abdicate their duty, sloughing it off onto yet another institution. And the only institution the child feels at home in is the hypercommercial one—all he wants is a Pepsi, just one Pepsi, and they wouldn't give it to him.

The song works musically as an anthem and lyrically as a rallying cry—along the same lines as the Who's "My Generation," but individualist. How to interpret the song is open to the listener, maybe even more so than most songs. You can cry, you can break things, or you can laugh. It is impossible to know if the singer is serious. The narrator writes his own name "Mike" in at the beginning, and this name is the same as the songwriter and singer. So the song would seem to be autobiographical.

But perhaps the narrator is trying to put one over on us. Maybe when he denies to his parents that he is on drugs, he is lying; heroin addicts, after all, crave the sugar in cola, and this is a familiar image. Maybe he is caricaturing the parent/child relationship—maybe we are supposed to both recognize it and recognize it as a cliché. Maybe when he quotes the parents' words, we are supposed to see them as expressing the typical antiyouth parental fears. And then there is the fact that the narrator is ultimately just a spoiled child demanding fulfillment: "All I wanted was a Pepsi," over and over again. In order to embrace the central message of the song, some listeners would have to distance themselves from this consumerist response. "Mike" may have wanted a Pepsi, but other punks were not so sure. The Middle Class rejected consumerism in "Out of Vogue," Black Flag mocked it in "TV Party," and the Descendents combined an ironic critique of suburbia, domesticity, and adolescent male identity formation in "Suburban Home":

> I want to be stereotyped
> I want to be classified
> I wanna be a clone
> I want a suburban home
> I wanna be masochistic
> I wanna be a statistic
> I don't want no hippie pad
> I want a house just like mom and dad.[57]

The oedipal tale of postsuburban punks was simultaneously an attempt to bring plot to the essentially plotless everyday, and to insert boys and their dads at the center of that plot. Mothers are conspicuously absent from hardcore punk lyrics. The plot was inevitably gendered, and postsuburban punk's critique of home and family links nicely with its emphasis on violence and its search for a personal politics.

5 BRATS in BATTALIONS

Hardcore Punk Rock, Violence, and the Politics of the Local

On St. Patrick's Day 1979, a Wednesday night, a wedding was held at the Elks Lodge in downtown Los Angeles, across the street from MacArthur Park. But that was not what brought the police there. At the same time, there were six hundred young people in the third-floor hall for a big punk rock gig, a little more than a year after the show that had served as L.A. punk's "coming out party." The Zeros, veteran punks from San Diego, had opened the night, followed by Portland's Wipers. The Plugz took the stage, and scheduled to follow were the Go-Gos (who had dyed their hair green for the occasion), the Alley Cats, and the current uncontested leaders of the L.A. scene, X. Instead, while the Plugz played, the Los Angeles Police Department (LAPD) arrived.

A couple of undercover cops entered first, in blue jeans, denim jackets, and flannel shirts, looking out of place not so much because of their fashion, but from their furtiveness, their suspicions, their defensive postures, which did not absorb but deflected the blows of other bodies slamming into them. It was obvious they were not used to this sort of thing and not completely open to it either. A few uniformed cops in riot gear entered the back of the hall, then left to the jeers of the crowd. They returned with reinforcements and began to clear out the seats that lined the side walls. Tito Larriva of the Plugz announced into the mike, "We'll play one that the pigs can pogo along with," and they slammed into their revved-up version of Ritchie Valens's "La Bamba" with Tito singing his revised lyrics,

"Surrados capitalistas, mas bien fascistas, yo no soy fascista, soy anarchista" ("Shit face capitalists, better known as fascists, I am not a fascist, I am an anarchist").[1] The singer's mike was cut off, and the Plugz continued with an instrumental version. Six cops began to rain blows with sticks on the head of one guy who was apparently too wasted to move upon command.

The LAPD had arrived in full force for a punk rock show. About fifty officers in full riot gear lined the stairway, one on each step, all the way up, past the wedding on the second floor to the third floor, where the last of the concert-goers were making their way out. Outside, cops with helmets, shields, and batons beat on punks under the glare of spotlights shining down from a helicopter hovering above the scene. Punks threw rocks, garbage, and whatever else they could find. It was the first time that L.A. punks were attacked in such a fashion by the police. It was, in fact, the first police assault on a rock show since a Pink Floyd concert at the Sports Arena in 1970. Punks had encountered the authorities before, and individual punks were always getting arrested. But they were usually arrested not for being punks, but for acting like punks—meaning they probably had done plenty to deserve it. While the Masque was frequently closed by the police and fire departments for code violations, the club had first attracted the attention of the police when one drunken punk lay down in the street and shouted "Fuck you pigs!"[2] At the Ramones' show at the Whisky in 1977, two cars from the Los Angeles Sheriff Department had pulled up to inspect the crowd outside, but the deputies had singled out a stoned, long-haired surfer-type for arrest, not a punk. At another punk show, the police had arrived, wandered around, even taken the stage, but they found no one to arrest, leading to a comical scene. Thereafter, whenever the police arrived at a show, there was a running joke in punk circles that they were actually the next band.[3]

It is unclear why the police came that night to the Elks Lodge in the way they did. Possibly a bottle was thrown in the lobby, and someone was cut. Maybe the management of the lodge called the police. Did the manager of the Plugz call, as Tito always suspected, in order to drum up some publicity for his band? But why bring the riot squad? And why were several punks beaten and bloodied, and eight arrested? One punk alleged a conspiracy of sorts, claiming that the beer and whiskey bottles he and his friends had emptied in the park across the street before the show had been picked up by the police before the riot in order to deprive the punks of weapons.[4] The response of the L.A. police at the Elks Lodge hearkens back to their response to the hippies who fought to abolish the curfew on Sunset Boulevard in 1966. Then, as in 1979, the LAPD, seeing young people out in public, dressed strangely and listening to weird music, sent in the riot squad to squash a perceived moral and civil threat.[5]

Ironically, the event was also a sign of how far punk had traveled along the road to respectability. Punk in its current incarnation was not usually seen as threatening, so it is remarkable that the police even came. The *Los Angeles Times* had two reporters there, who defended the punks and took their side, claiming that the violence was instigated entirely by the police. They did not bury the story, returning to it over the following weeks. The *Times* music critics had by now almost completely embraced the local punk scene; while not giving it enormous amounts of newsprint, they generally wrote positive reviews. The fact that two *Times* reporters attended the show attests to L.A. punk rock's acceptance, signaling a blurring of the line between subculture and dominant culture.[6]

The police riot, however, served to draw that line more firmly. In some ways it legitimated the L.A. punk scene among punks and punks-to-be; the "Elks Lodge Massacre," as it was hyperbolically termed, became a historic event that took on mythic status.[7] In such songs as the Gears' "Elks Lodge Blues" and the Angry Samoans' "Pig," the riot is referred to as the event that transformed punk. After that moment, L.A. punk took place in the world, rather than in some isolated subcultural scene. Punk was now political, not so much by its ideology as by its context. Up til now, punk had largely avoided the scrutiny of the authorities. As Dez Cadena of Black Flag noted, "It was cool in LA all the way up to Elks Lodge." Said bandmate Chuck Dukowski, "People were doing absolutely nothing and the cops came in and started dusting people off. The odd thing about these riots is that the cops are scared of it. They're scared of what they see in the music, what they see happening when people do it, the energy in it. They're scared of what might happen if someone like that had a direction and focused that energy."[8]

The stakes had changed. People who previously might have had no reason to be attracted to punk were now drawn by the idea that it seemed to make authorities scared. The Elks Lodge Massacre occurred at a pivotal moment in the history of L.A. punk, just as the music was gaining a degree of mainstream legitimacy, as more and more teens and young adults in the outlying areas were paying attention. The moment when punk became violent was, then, the exact moment when punk in Southern California became political because the context for punk was now social, not merely musical. Perhaps fittingly, the most famous photograph of the Elks Lodge Massacre was of the stitched-up head of a highly respected member of the Middle Class.

The police riot served to close one era of L.A. punk and foreshadow another—an era that would be filled with major demonstrations of police strength and violence at punk rock shows. The seeds had been sown for a redefinition of punk rock. Punk already meant different things than it was supposed to. Kids were already calling themselves punks who had no right to, and in places no punk should ever admit to frequenting. By June 1980, even the *Times* was vehemently denouncing punk rock. But this was punk with a new face, ready to fight at a moment's notice.

In the years following the Elks Lodge incident, violent conflict was inaugurated by police, punk haters, and punks alike. To outsiders, hardcore punk seemingly represented a rejection of the dominant values of the local society. Chuck Dukowski may have been correct that punk was viewed as a threat to the established order. The responses of the police and media certainly suggest that they saw punk as a social threat even before punks did. Punks in Huntington Beach and throughout the area were pulled over by the police and had their picture taken for the notorious punk rock file, while organized gangs of antipunk vigilantes looked for punks to fight in the streets.[9] Soon it seemed that there was hardly a gig at which the police didn't show up, batons at the ready.

Violence, Dominant Culture, and Hardcore Punk Rock

Over the next few years, a minor media panic developed in Los Angeles and nationally about the new punk called "hardcore." In the summer of 1980, the *Los Angeles Times* printed an exposé by Patrick Goldstein describing a hardcore scene rife with violence, vandalism, self-mutilation, and clashes with police. Punk violence was blamed mostly on organized suburban and beach-area hardcore gangs who wreaked destruction both outside the clubs and in—particularly on the dance floor. Punks, Goldstein wrote, "don't just dance anymore. They mug each other. It's part of a new 'dance' craze called the Slam, whose popularity, especially with organized gangs of punk youths, has led to numerous incidents of violence at many area clubs. The accounts of senseless violence, vandalism and even mutilation at some area rock clubs read like reports from a war zone."[10] The article signaled a new attitude toward punk in the mainstream media resulting from the changes punk had undergone.

While punk rock had excited a media frenzy in 1976 and 1977 in tabloid-mad England, until 1979 it had never been portrayed in the United States as anything more than an imported oddity that had failed to catch on. By the late seventies, punk had even gained a certain degree of musical acceptance, especially in Los Angeles.[11] Now, however, the mainstream media changed their approach to the homegrown hardcore scene. A variety of films, television shows, and press reports introduced hardcore to a gradually widening audience. Science fiction and exploitation films such as *Class of 1984*, *Road Warrior*, and *Return of the Living Dead* were among the first to feature the hardcore punk visual style of leather, spikes, chains, and mohawks. The independent films *Suburbia* and *Repo Man* employed the hardcore punk attitude and setting for offbeat narratives that simultaneously sympathized with and exploited hardcore. *People* magazine introduced slam dancing to readers across the country. On TV, hardcore punk made ideal fodder for newsmagazines, audience participation talk shows, and cop shows. *The Phil Donahue Show* invited hardcore punks and an organization called Parents of Punkers to debate the causes and consequences of hardcore. The crime dramas *CHiPs* and *Quincy, M.E.* each devoted an episode to the hardcore scene, which was portrayed as corrupting youth, destroying families, and causing violence throughout Middle America. On *Hunter*, Sergeant Rick Hunter, played by former pro football player Fred Dryer, sported a blue mohawk while infiltrating a hardcore punk gang led by a biker played by another former pro football player, John Matuszak. Punk even showed up in the comic books, as Jughead Jones from the *Archie* series went undercover as a punk for the Riverdale High School newspaper.[12]

Hardcore punks in Southern California had strong opinions about their portrayal by the media. In a sense, they depended on the media condemnation for their identity. But they claimed that the *Times* had misrepresented them in its article about violence in hardcore punk, and they reviled Goldstein, who was accused of inventing the term "slam dancing."[13]

focuses on the activity of consumption—the most daily of activities in our world—as a type of usage, and thus of production, calling attention to "the tactics of consumption, the ingenious ways in which the weak make use of the strong, thus lend[ing] a political dimension to everyday practices." This is explicitly a way of seeing how the dominated in society put to use the products, words, and ideas imposed by the dominant economic, linguistic, and ideological orders. Importantly, for de Certeau domination occurs not simply along race, gender, or class lines but through the articulation of power in spatial practices. These practices make almost everyone, even middle-class punk rockers in Southern California, potentially part of the dominated; as de Certeau writes, "Marginality is becoming universal."[22]

As youth in postsuburbia, punks were marginalized in specific ways. According to de Certeau's theory of everyday life, strategy belongs to those in power, firmly rooted in a place; tactics are for those marginalized, homeless, who have to play the game of everyday life within the rules set by those in power. Poaching is how the marginalized best insert themselves into the landscape, into history: "Everyday life invents itself by poaching in countless ways on the property of others."[23] De Certeau's use of the notions of property, space, strategy vs. tactics, and poaching are useful in understanding punk rock, even if they are a bit reductive. The opposition de Certeau makes between tactics and strategies is too simplistic, and punks used both. Further, this dichotomy too easily creates a sense of everyday life as simply a reflection of the struggle between the empowered and the powerless. But the analogy works well for hardcore punk rockers, because their violent responses to the postsuburban landscape reflected just the military analogy de Certeau draws. While Henri Lefebvre argues that "brutal assertiveness" provides inadequate compensation for the "deep and multiple frustrations" engendered by youth's "marginal everyday life," hardcore punks attempted just this type of compensation.[24]

If in postsuburbia power is exercised through space, hardcore punks attempted to intercede in their communities through spatial practices. In response to their position in the consumerist postsuburban environment, punks acted tactically in ways that both challenged and reproduced the dominant ideologies of postsuburbia. The punk subculture mirrored the decentralized nature of postsuburbia, and reflected the nature of power and politics in Orange County. In articulating a tactical politics, punks rejected both consumerism and, importantly, a universal model of youth culture which had motivated an earlier generation. Their conceptions of citizenship and community were localized, fragmented, even ephemeral.

In contrast to the search for stability ("strategic" responses) discussed in the last chapter, punks also interceded, as de Certeau would say, tactically, locally, at the level of consumption, on the dominant institutions and discourses of society.[25] Many of the activities of postsuburban punks can be seen as a kind of poaching: of appropriation and inscription. The mere act of dressing punk was an act of appropriation, of the type of bricolage that Dick Hebdige describes of London punk.[26] The Southern California hardcore punk style also appropriated from local cultures—Chicano gang style and especially surfing and skateboarding. Punk at the beach intertwined with surf culture. While partly a rejection, it also transformed.

Some surfers became punks. They redesigned their surfboards to be considerably shorter, with two or three fins instead of one, for easier maneuverability on the small waves which were the norm; "aggro" surfers now "shredded" the wave, rather than simply respond to and mesh with nature as the hippie surfers had.[27] Surfing served not as a means of getting in touch with Mother Nature, but of dominating her.[28] Skateboarding, similarly, inscribed punks into the landscape, as both the (emptied) pools of suburbia and the (surveilled) office parks of technoburbia presented perfect, if dangerous, opportunities for poaching on someone else's space.[29]

Punks also poached living, business, and performance spaces by squatting or renting abandoned industrial spaces. Clubs continually opened and closed, often in different locations scattered all over the Southern California area, connected by the criss-crossing lines of the freeways.[30] Most often punks played parties or in clubs and halls that only lasted for a few months, often shut down because of the violence. And even this violence may be viewed as inscription and poaching.

Punks did not own the streets or the malls or the corridors in the high school. They could get beaten up for looking punk, even arrested or photographed by the police.[31] As the Battalion of Saints sang, "Cops are out, I run and hide / They're looking for me, / And I don't know why."[32] One way for punks to take power was to walk down the streets in packs or (occasionally) organized gangs. The tactic was defensive, in the sense of always being ready to defend against violent attacks by so-called rednecks or jocks; but beyond the military tactical analogy, the other tactics had to do with identity, with taking space in order to create a self and a community, to be the "Boys in the Brigade," as the Youth Brigade sang. Gangs like the La Mirada Punks fought regularly against both the La Mirada Stoners (nonpunks) and other punk gangs, mingling identity and community concerns, both defining identity through insider/outsider distinctions and contesting the definition of "punk."[33] Punk gangs, both loose and organized, poached on alien turf, and organized themselves into alternative communities. Punk poaching reflected its politics and the larger arena of politics in Southern California.

"The Watts riot of the middle classes"

The politics of Southern California were conservative through most of the twentieth century. In Los Angeles, the right-wing "Otis-Chandler dynasty" of the *Times* headed up a downtown establishment which competed since the 1920s with a more liberal, Democratic Westside leadership for hegemony.[34] Orange County voted Republican in every presidential election in the century, with the exception of the Depression years 1932 and 1936. Further, with the establishment of the John Birch Society and the county's pivotal role in swinging the 1964 California Republican primary to Barry Goldwater, Orange County was established as the standard bearer of what Kevin Phillips called in 1970 "the emerging Republican majority." The new "populist conservatism" of Orange County placed it no longer on the outside of mainstream politics but firmly on the leading edge, so much so that one scholar could title his 1974 book on "the future of American politics," *As Orange Goes.*[35]

The politics of Southern California in the 1970s were increasingly conservative, and increasingly centered around issues of homeowner self-defense. No longer were homeowners concerned with the establishment of the suburban ideal. The conservative politics of the region developed in the homeowners associations that began to oppose further development, in defense of their property values and lifestyles.[36] The "politics of exclusion,"[37] a national phenomenon, were especially pronounced in the region as developers strived to fill in any open spaces. At the same time, locally the price of real estate—and accompanying property taxes—exploded.[38]

Within the context of the post-1968 conservative turn in American politics, economic uncertainty and stagflation, and myriad local issues involving growth and racial and class conflict, Southern California homeowners were hit with exorbitant property tax increases. In the mid-1960s Los Angeles County Assessor Philip E. Watson began a campaign to reform property values and tax rates. In response to an irrational, scandalous, corrupt, probusiness, and unequal system, Watson's office planned to assess all property at 25 percent of market price. Unfortunately, and ironically, in what Clarence Lo calls "the misdirected efforts of progressive reformers," the new policy shifted the property tax burden onto homeowners, making them particularly "vulnerable to the inflation of home prices, which would automatically trigger higher assessments."[39] By the mid-1970s, both Los Angeles and Orange counties, in attempting to rationalize their property tax systems, were using, in addition, computers and regression analysis to reappraise hundreds of thousands of properties. While higher property value assessments would potentially increase the wealth and status of homeowners, the tax rates were crippling, especially for retirees in the San Fernando Valley and Orange County. Not only were property values, and their assessed tax rates, exponentially higher, but the new system was so bureaucratic that government officials were completely unresponsive to the frustrations of homeowners. Lo argues that it was this frustration, what he calls the "frustrated advantage" of the upper middle class—with its "advantages in class, status, and/or political power in some arenas, but relative powerlessness in other arenas"—which led the homeowners' associations to organize and revolt against "unresponsive big government."[40]

The most visible manifestation of the new politics of the region (and the nation) was this homeowner revolt which culminated in the tax-protest measure Proposition 13 in 1978, for which homeowners, particularly in the San Fernando Valley, provided the "shock troops."[41] Claiming that "many of the actors in this drama were the direct beneficiaries of one of the largest mass windfalls of wealth in history," Mike Davis describes the conflict in his most elegant prose: "The folk maxim that gaunt men rebel while fat men sleep was neatly reversed by the historic suburban protests of 1976–9. In face of a massive inflationary redistribution of wealth, it was the haves, not the have-nots, who raised their pikes in the great tax revolt and its kindred school and growth protests."[42] But the crabgrass-roots political movement was not only inspired by the sentiment of "I've got mine, so to Hell with the rest of you."[43] Homeowners simply could not pay their property taxes. Their anger over this issue combined with the Supreme Court order to integrate the Los Angeles County schools through busing, with "a host of new growth-related complaints," and with an increasing frustration with unresponsive, bureaucratic, and fragmented governments to sweep the state.[44] While the campaign initially focused only on residential property, not commercial, Proposition 13 limited taxes to 1 percent of all property. The campaign had begun in homeowners' associations in the middle-class suburbs of the San Fernando Valley, but was "hijacked" by upper middle-class homeowners and big business interests. It was this development which led to the upward redistribution of wealth with Proposition 13.

The politics of hardcore punks reflected the general tenor of politics in postsuburbia and in California more generally in the 1970s and 1980s. As the region sprouted more and more gated residential communities, malls with panoptic surveillance systems, and the office towers of "Fortress L.A.," punks, who had no land, property, or public space to call their own, poached on the symbols and space of the dominant culture. As the "excluded," hardcore punks in turn fashioned their own politics based upon exclusion and the limited aims of defensible space—a politics with violence at its core.

"Bored boys with nothing to do"

By the fall of 1980, hardly a show went by without some major conflagration, whether ignited by punks or police. On September 19, the brand-new Hideaway Club was set to open up with a show by Black Flag, Geza X and the Mommymen, Circle Jerks, the Descendents, the Stains, and Mad Society (continuing after hours with performances by UXA, Saccharine Trust, and the Minutemen). More than twelve hundred punks showed up. More than three hundred were still waiting outside as the first band went on, and only two bands had played by 1 A.M. Poor planning, bad ventilation, and inept door management brought violence. The punks broke down the door to get in (using a car as a battering ram), then broke it down again later to get out. Inside, they kicked holes in all the newly sheet-rocked walls, finally knocking down the wall dividing the main hall from the lobby, where kids were still waiting to pay and get in. The punks

Black Flag, with frontman Henry Rollins at center.
Photograph © by Ed Arnaud.

trashed the club, and the police then showed up and closed down the show.[45]

A few weeks later, on October 8, a Wednesday night, Black Flag and DOA were scheduled to play two sets at the Whisky a Go-Go, a rare hardcore gig at the club. As the audience from the very intense first show filtered out onto Sunset Boulevard, while the line of several hundred ticket holders for the second show waited to get in, a single Sheriff's Department car pulled up. Cops and punks exchanged words. A punk lofted a Budweiser at the patrol car. The officers radioed for reinforcements. The club owner cancelled the second show and, one witness reported, "hell broke loose with bottles raining from all directions."[46] Another punk described the scene: "Within minutes, the intersections a block above and below on Sunset were barricaded by police cars, traffic was diverted down side streets and no less than twenty-three cop cars came tearing up, lights and sirens blazing. An unmarked blue car unloaded four cops in full riot gear, and one of them got out clutching a shotgun tightly to his chest. The cops deployed and began chasing people up and down the street."[47]

The worst episode was yet to come. On Friday, October 24, nearly a thousand punks showed up for a show by Black Flag, the Skrews, and UXA at Baces Hall, a club in East Hollywood with a capacity of three hundred. San Francisco punk Jonathan Formula, visiting the southland to research an article on the new hardcore punk scene, reported,

> The police seemed to have prepared for this one in advance, as a pha-lanx of riot-equipped officers confronted the hundreds of kids unable to get in off the street. Whereas the Whiskey incident was a punk rout, with cops hastily conferring about tactics before chasing people around in every direction, at Bace's the kids stood up against the men in blue for as long as they could, with rocks and bottles flying out from behind the front lines. With a military precision reminiscent of the nefarious Elk's Lodge blitz of recent years, the formation of cops pulled on black leather gloves, pulled out riot sticks from their belts in unison, and took a few steps towards the crowd in formation before breaking ranks and chasing down singled-out targets from the groups of kids attempt-ing to escape down the squad-car blockaded street. Inside the club, the cops were held back temporarily by the promoter, who told them that a riot would ensue if the plug were pulled. Halfway through Black Flag's set, probably coinciding with the arrival of reinforcements, the cops decided it was time to clear the house, and Black Flag continued to play right up until their instruments were yanked out of their hands, at which point they sat down on stage to avoid providing any excuse for skullcrackery.[48]

The police were becoming increasingly zealous and organized in their violence against punks. But much of the violence also resulted from the growing popularity of hardcore. As new kids converted to punk every day, the audiences outgrew the clubs, surprising the bookers and owners who underestimated hardcore's drawing power. Although Black Flag had warned the promoter at the Whisky about the size and nature of their crowd, he couldn't believe the band would actually sell out two shows on a Wednesday night. The woman who booked the Hideaway gig had been pleasantly surprised at the success of her first promotion of a punk show a few weeks before, but she seriously underestimated the management skills that would be necessary to handle ten bands and over a thousand punks.

Some of the violence came from the punks themselves, of course. After all, punks were violent, weren't they? Well, earlier punks would claim the violence was simulated, and they were more likely to hurt themselves and get beaten up by others, than to hurt each other or go out in gangs beating up hippies. When they did get bruised and battered, it was most likely because they had drunkenly fallen down the stairs leading down into the Masque. In those early days, female punk cliques battling in the hallways of the Canterbury were the main source of violence. "I've probably punched everyone I know," admitted Hollywood punk Pat Smear, the Germs' guitarist, interviewed in the film *Decline of Western Civilization*. "But then I ran because I'm basically a coward."

Hardcore punks, in contrast, liked to inflict damage, both on the dance floor and everywhere else. The new scene was centered in Huntington Beach, and the punks from there, known as HBs, represented a new breed of punk. They liked to fight. Not all of them, of course, and some came to punk for the music, or the punk ideology, or just getting wasted. But from the beginning, violence lay at the core of the new beach scene. Musically and stylistically, friction developed between the Day-Glo surf punk set (centered on the band the Crowd) and the leather, boots, and chains crowd from Surfside. But they would all play parties together, fight each other, and unite to beat the shit out of hippies who invaded their backyard parties. "You might think we were violent," one punk recalled. "I guess we were, violence was a daily thing. The more rotten or fucked you were, the cooler you were. We pushed the limits—sometimes they snapped. It was about energy, outrageousness, and anarchy. It was about shock value. . . . Punk rock made us feel alive. . . . You never knew when a carload of hippies, jocks, or vigilante construction worker dads would decide to jump out of a car and beat the shit out of you. Walking alone was always a thrill."[49]

For hardcore punks, violence made a daily thing into a thrill, the mundane, extraordinary—particularly within the context of the post-suburban landscape, where pedestrians were isolated and vulnerable. This was certainly one way to beat boredom, to feel alive. Jack Grisham, lead singer of the pioneering Vicious Circle (later T.S.O.L.), admitted to becoming a punk for the fights, not the music. "You know . . . just have a few beers and get in a fight," he said. "See we were big guys. Everyone would fuck with punks, but we were big enough so that when people said, 'Fuck you, punks', we would go, 'No, fuck you, let's go,' then we'd stop and fight 'em all. There were all these battles going on. The metalheads who hated punks, the cops thought we were freaks. We were fighting all the hippies, all the bikers, everybody. Every where I went. Going to the liquor store was a big event."[50] Again, the mundane became extraordinary in the context of punk rock, and the mundane landscape of everyday life in postsuburbia was turned into something exceptional. The most basic of events for a rebellious youth, going to the liquor store to steal beer or convince someone over twenty-one to purchase it, became a "big event," a chance to fight. The fights were not so much over turf, as with traditional urban gangs, because punks claimed no turf as their own outside of their clubs. All space belonged to someone else, so all space was potentially an arena for tactical violence with no larger purpose than the fighting itself. Hardcore punks felt no need to claim any larger goal.

Hardcore punks took a part of the punk philosophy and distilled it down to the core of rage. It was expressed in Black Flag's music: the "soundtrack for Armageddon," as one Bay Area punk described it.[51] It was expressed in the lyrics to such songs as "Nervous Breakdown," "I've Had It," and "No Values." Combined with that rage was a redefined punk version of anarchy. If early Hollywood punk had derived much of its stated political philosophy from the Situationists, via London punk, the new punks took the punk code words and refashioned them.[52] Above all, hardcore punk anarchy meant no rules. And no rules to a teenage boy newly turned punk meant the freedom to get wasted, hang out with your bros, and break things up. As one "Aitch Bee" punk remembered: "Around each band there were usually a couple nuts. In some cases (V.C., T.S.O.L., The Outsiders, The Slashers) the nuts were in the band. We all drank a lot. The more we drank and got high, the crazier it would get. We were seventeen, loaded and invincible."[53] As the Circle Jerks sang, adopting a youth slogan that went back at least to the fifties, "Live fast / Die young."

Unlike Hollywood punk, which had focused on a set of institutions—a club, a zine or two, a slew of bands and their friends—the Huntington Beach scene became delineated by bands. The bands all had their own groups of friends and followers who traveled with them from gig to gig, party to party. The media and the police labeled these groups as "gangs," and there was some truth to the accusation. Punks would deny it, and the groups were never organized or hierarchical, but "every band had their bros and bros stick together." Sometimes they took a name without a band such as the Wayward Cains: "You needed to be a punk and a bit nuts. No rules, no ranks, no leaders, just anarchy where you could make it or find it."[54] Built into the hardcore show was the "dance floor" of barely (and not always) controlled violence. Jonathan Formula described "the boiling, roiling, leaping, writhing, frenzied crowd": "I couldn't focus my eyes on the kids thrashing down below, I could only see a huge, bubbling mass of boots, bandannas, chains, black and red and faded blue, contorted faces, crazy colors and chromed spikes, swirling like a colony of angry young urban microbes under a microscope. It was like looking into the face of a tidal wave."[55] Spot, Black Flag's sound engineer and occasional bouncer, recalled the scene at the Fleetwood, a large Redondo Beach punk venue: "The HBs were all leather jackets, chains, macho, bloodlust, and bravado, and exhibited blatantly stupid military behavior. It was never a dull moment. There was a mass brawl every five minutes and as stage manager I had a chance to witness them all. Sure, the fights were quite pointless but they were determined to happen."[56]

By 1980, the letters sections of all the zines were filled with debates about the meaning of punk violence. While many of the letters decried the supposedly false media stereotype, more often the debate over violence cohered around questions of who was and who was not a real punk. One punk wrote to *Flipside* in 1981:

> I'm writing this letter to all the people who keep writing in complaining about the "new punks" of the "HB's." You keep saying that they are cloning themselves and that they are quoat "passe" and that somebody has to change to make the quoat 'scene' better, well FUCK OFF! . . . And you call the new people trendies because they don't wear what your wearing. Well your just part of that new trend: The individual trend. . . . P.S. This fighting has got to stop, punk vs. punk is BULLSHIT!! Those of you who go to gigs and fight are gonna end up getting your asses kicked in the end. Besides it's not worth it. We all have the same basic idea, so if your gonna fight, fight the hippies, besides you can grab their hair.[57]

After the Goldstein article, the debate raged over whether real punks beat up other punks. Both sides claimed the status of real for themselves. And both agreed, for the most part, that beating up hippies was acceptable, perhaps even necessary. Another letter, from "the silent majority" accused *Flipside* of giving too much positive attention to Huntington Beach punks, who did not deserve it because "HB's go out of their way to beat someone up, or knife a person. . . . They seem to think violence is cool or scars on your arm look tough."[58] Hudley from *Flipside* responded, "Mindless violence is fucked, but that's just a reality we have to deal with right now!!!!" Again, this violence was "determined to happen." Steve Stiph editorialized in his *Outcry* zine:

> And why is it that certain assholes who are always fighting seem to have a following of people who think they're cool and look up to them. Could be because most of these "blind sheep" are wimps who need "gang mentality" to achieve a feeling of power. . . . There do seem to be some thickheads who think it's their call in life to control the action in "the pit" at local punk gigs. If you drive somebody off the dance floor or beat them up because they don't "look cool," then you're not only a jerk—you're also a conformist! That's right—you can have a mohawk (or a skinhead, or blue hair or whatever . . .) and still be a conformist.[59]

These kinds of exchanges were, next to the accounts of the music, the dominant material in zines. A common argument was that punks should unite against oppressive outsiders because they generally shared the same values. But as the steady stream of letters to zines demonstrated, not everyone agreed. Many held the view that violent punks were not real punks, but rather posers and clones. It was the same line of "reasoning" used by the violent punks to choose their victims.

Two songs by the Adolescents from opposite sides of their first album indicate the conflict over violence within hardcore. On the a-side, in "Wrecking Crew," the singer Tony growls and howls, "We're just a wrecking crew / Bored boys with nothing to do." When the "excitement level" is "zero" and you "can't find a girl, cos they're all out chasing heroes," you find "an enemy to beat" and "overturn cars and rip up the street." Tony proclaims proudly, "I'm tired of being a peaceful citizen / Noise and destruction are in my vision." On the flipside of the album, "Rip It Up" condemns this very vision: "Like *Clockwork Orange*, a bit of twenty on one / Breaking heads don't sound like much fun." Tony issues a challenge to his audience in personal terms: "Do you think you're tough, when you rip it up?"

"Wrecking Crew" sings the praises of the pure joy of a teenager who feels invincible, the joy of being able to get in a fight with a very good shot at winning ("safety in numbers"), of submerging one's identity in a group. The purpose of punk rock is no more than to alleviate boredom through violence. On the flipside of the album, the Adolescents condemn gang violence within punk. This was not simply a case of cognitive dissonance, or teenage stupidity. The sentiments of both songs were necessary to hardcore punk. "Wrecking Crew" presents the attractions of punk to a young male in postsuburban Southern California. "Rip It Up" presents the problems that arise once someone has embraced the punk scene—no one is safe from attack. "Just to kill boredom / makes no sense": in other words, there must be something more to punk rock. The song makes a vague call "to unite," as did many of the letters published in zines, but there was nothing explicitly to unite over other than the music and the scene. The music itself was not a strong enough focus for hardcore punks—since punk was supposed to be about something more than music—and the "scene" was defined primarily by its violence. So the song can come up with no solution, no way out of the contradiction. Finally, by chanting "GOTTA RIP IT UP" over and over throughout the song, the Adolescents leave every possibility that the antiviolence message of the song could be lost altogether on the audience. The "wrecking crew" and *A Clockwork Orange*-style violence highlight the limits of the hardcore punk vision.

Hardcore cannot be understood in terms of any specific political agenda on the Right or the Left. Hardcore punks in Southern California were usually vaguely "anarchist" or "leftist," but most of them disavowed any explicit political position. The violence helped punks fashion themselves as a subculture in opposition to a dominant culture. Tony from the Adolescents remembers watching from the stage as two rival groups of punks fought in the audience, came together to fight the police who charged through to break it up, and then, as the end of the police wedge passed through toward the stage, recombined behind the police to fight each other again.[60] Contrary to the Adolescents' admonition, "We're not the background to your stupid fights," hardcore bands often did serve as such a background.

Punk violence was just as often directed within as without. Punks often practiced a form of self-mutilation of punks called "carving," which entailed slicing one's body with a razor blade. The cutting was a type of writing on the body, akin to tattooing, and a rejection of the dominant Southern Californian ideal of the beautiful body; it claimed the body as one's own space, removed it from the realm of commodification. It also restated the body as the site of abuse. Henry Rollins, the lead singer of Black Flag, describes numerous instances of self-mutilation in his diary. "9.22.84 Guernville CA: . . . Gig went well. A lot of people showed up. I found a small room to hang out in before the show. I found a piece of broken glass and started slamming it into my chest. Blood started flying all over the place. It felt good to feel pure pain. Helped me get perspective."[61] Rollins performed this action sober and presumably in control. While there was a tradition of self-mutilation in rock 'n' roll, especially in punk rock, the act was always performed as theater, even as a ritualized sacrifice. For Rollins, however, carving was not about performance—it was part of his everyday life. "The owner of the club came and saw me and bailed fast. He must have thought I was crazy. Like I give a fuck about what he thinks." But Rollins does care. The owner is essential to the story as proof that Rollins is different from others, that he could reach something "pure, direct and simple to understand."[62] Carving was a part of everyday life, and it was one way Rollins established his identity as a real person in a hyperreal world.

Hardcore punk was in one way a pursuit of reality. Bands such as Black Flag and the Minutemen valorized touring above all else, as it signified hard work and a rejection of consumerism (although the Minutemen's philosophy of "jamming econo" was far more explicitly political and anti-consumerist, valorizing the "idea of scarcity").[63] Recordings were made as a way to get people to come to shows, reversing the priority of the normal rock business, in which touring was undertaken simply to promote an already recorded product. Rollins's tour diary from his stint with Black Flag in the early eighties is filled with often numbingly mundane details of driving, driving, and more driving, of hours spent trying to fall asleep while wedged in the back of the van between speaker cabinets. Rollins chronicles the sound checks, the interviews, the meals, the nights spent on people's floors, the fighting—between band members, among audience members, and between band and audience—and the shows that kept it all going. Rock 'n' roll stood for hardness, and hardcore meant reality—it was the hardness of touring which separated Black Flag from the rest of society—and from most (to him, inauthentic) punks: "Black Flag was on a work ethic that I had never experienced and have never seen since. Greg, Chuck and their nonstop roadie Mugger were the hardest working people I had ever seen. If you ever made a noise about anything, Mugger would just start laughing and say something like, 'This isn't Van Halen! Get it happening!'. . . I learned what hard work was with Black Flag."[64]

Black Flag's adoption of the punk animosity toward hippies reflected not so much disgust with the music business, in contrast to earlier punks, but instead disgust with the consumerist ethos, an ethos that led people to accept their fate.[65] Black Flag rejected the foundational distinction between work and leisure in postmodern consumer society. To them, touring represented the refusal to accept the safe suburban home, an inscription ("creepy crawling" they called it, after Charles Manson) on the American landscape with the objective to leave their mark and move on, not conquer markets or the masses.[66] Black Flag's entry into everyday life both rejected and replicated parts of the dominant value system of postsuburbia, but without making any explicit political statement. Bass player Chuck Dukowski defined the anarchic politics of their music: "My definition of it is, a commitment to change, no system. Cuz the world really is anarchy. But a person committed to it is committed to destruction of the status quo."[67] But beyond that, there was no specified agenda. Black Flag described their songs, like so many of the postsuburban punk bands did, as personal, not directly political: "They deal with everyday things that may happen to you," according to vocalist Dez Cadena.[68] Added Greg Ginn, the band's guitarist and chief songwriter: "[A] lot of our politics is in our sound, but not just on the surface. . . . There is no one solution, musically, politically or ideologically. . . . A preachy political song can have less impact than your actions."[69]

Black Flag's stance on punk violence reflected their apolitical politics and their staunch individualism. Ginn was producing electronic components for a living when he decided to try to put a band together after hearing the Ramones in 1976.[70] Because of their musical experience and the fact that they were already producing their own recordings and performances, Black Flag became the standard-bearer of the beach punk phenomenon. They quickly became the most popular band among the new crowd of punks. They were banned from every club in the area because of the often legitimate fear of violence at their shows. They were harassed by police and forced out of several living and office sites.

The debate over punk violence raged both within the scene and between hardcore punks and the institutions of the dominant culture. "Whose Responsibility?" asked a mainstream rock newspaper, prompted specifically by Black Flag's refusal to speak out, either from the stage or in the press, against the violence at their concerts. Punks and their defenders responded in a variety of ways to what they considered unfair treatment in the press. The owner of one punk club argued that bands and promoters should join together to keep the violent element out. A punk from Hermosa Beach blamed the rock press for noticing Black Flag only when there was violence involved. Another defended Black Flag's position as artists and claimed the violence was not being perpetrated by "real" punks: "Black Flag shouldn't have to discourage their crowd from violence. They are musicians not policemen. The majority of what you call Huntington Beach surf-punks are actually . . . people who don't know or respect what the scene is really about."[71] But the Huntington Beach punks were violent—proudly and unabashedly so—from the very beginning of their scene.

Black Flag neither condemned the violence surrounding them, nor articulated a defense of their own position. Their silence signaled not simply an acceptance of the violence, but a specific political stance that reflected their social environment and time. By claiming that they hated authority, they could refuse to assume it. They used the black flag as a symbol of anarchy to free themselves from the leadership position of the rock star. But their music and performance *was* designed to make something happen. Antipolice songs like "Revenge" and "Police Story" and lyrics like "I've got no values / nothing to say / I've got no values / might as well blow you away" confirmed their violent image. But the band did not defend their audience either. In fact, by the time Rollins joined as the fourth and final lead singer in mid-1981, the band was aiming its assault as much at its own audience as at the world outside. Rollins made it a point to separate himself from the punk rock posers who came to his shows. In this, of course, he was little different from other punks who

debated the conformity of the scene. In fact, the contestation, fragmentation, and violence within the scene provide the key to understanding this
specific subculture, and more generally, the position of youth in 1970s
postsuburban society.

Postsuburban punk rockers refused a unitary position, rejecting
universals and even strategic thinking, in reflection of their position in
a postmodern, postsuburban world. In declining to speak against punk
violence, Black Flag refused to set themselves up as leaders of a movement. Unlike the previous generation's leaders, and even unlike punks in
other locales, they did not attempt to centralize in pursuit of either power
or ideals. In Northern California's Bay Area, a small group of punks established bands, zines, and record labels with the explicit purpose of providing the central institutions for what they hoped would be an international
youth movement. In postsuburban Southern California, however, punks
preferred to fight over the meaning, fashion, and sound of punk rather
than attempt a politics modeled on an ideal of "youth culture."

Youth violence was not a new social development, of course. In the
1950s, mainstream society had been shocked by the violence of "juvenile
delinquents." In the 1960s, however, most youth had seen themselves
as peaceful—as passive consumers of the Pepsi Generation, as agents of
social change modeling themselves on the nonviolent direct action of the
civil rights movement, or as hippies embracing peace and love. When violence broke out, it was thought to come from the authorities: the military
in Vietnam, redneck sheriffs in the South, or the police in cities across
America. When the Chicago police cracked the heads of demonstrators in
1968, young people chanted "The whole world is watching," assuming that
their peaceful demeanor brought them sanction in the eyes of the public.
Youth identity and community were maintained with a peaceful vision,
often defined explicitly in opposition to a violent mainstream.

In the 1970s and 1980s, a subculture of youth once again saw violence
as a viable way to define identity and community. Ronald Reagan's assault
on the "Evil Empire," centered in the military-industrial complexes of
Southern California, offered a model of violence, and the contentiousness
of the local homeowners' tax revolt, antibusing movement, and residential slow growth movement emphasized defensiveness and the sanctity of
borders: the politics of exclusion. The politics of hardcore punk reflected
the local political tactics in Southern California. After the Elks Lodge riot,

violence was attractive to the new breed of punk, offering justification.

Like the Black Power movement after 1965, or fragments of the New Left after 1968, the violence of the authorities against a subculture or social movement seemed to justify a violent response. With hardcore punk rock, however, violence was not targeted simply at the "establishment" or authority figures; it was endemic to the "scene" and to the creation of that scene.

Conclusion

PUNK ROCK changed OUR LIVES

Punk Identity and the Creation of Mass Subculture

Hardcore was white music. I can think of no better way to say it. Musically, the sound stripped out nearly all rhythm and even melody. Generally, the only variation occurred in tempo. Ideologically, though, while many hardcore punks adopted the skinhead look, there was no organized fascism or white supremacy movement among Southern California punks.[1]

To be sure, enough punks sported swastikas (following the pioneering Sid Vicious and Siouxsie Sioux of London), to cause Phranc—the "Jewish lesbian folksinger" formerly of the riveting and frightening industrial punk noise band Nervous Gender (sample lyric: "Jesus was a cocksucking jew from Galilee / Jesus was just like me / A homosexual nymphomaniac! / A homosexual nymphomaniac!")—to pen a song called "Take Off Your Swastikas." Similarly, San Francisco's Dead Kennedys, who gigged frequently in So Cal, sang a rousing "Nazi Punks Fuck Off." Hardcore punks often behaved and looked like fascist stormtroopers, and touring racist British bands played to large crowds, but race was at most a minor theme for hardcore punks. So while Black Flag's "White Minority" seemed to lament the day in the near future when "all the rest will be the majority. . . . We're all gonna die," their singer at the time when they debuted the song was Latino.

Early Hollywood punks had freely adopted Patti Smith's "Rock N Roll Nigger," especially when Black Randy and the Metrosquad were playing their funk-punk hybrid in songs like "Idi Amin" with the delightful rhyme, "Idi Amin / I am your fan." There was a certain "white negro" identification with blacks as the oppressed, a "love and theft" of African American culture.[2] The band Dred Scott pasted flyers around their town with the famous slave's visage. In "Los Angeles" X used the N word, but not derogatory slang terms for the other groups they sang of. The Controllers used the lyrics "I wanna get v.d. / be real mean / I wanna be black and look like Idi Amin" to propel an oldstyle rock 'n' roll rave-up in "Do the Uganda." These lyrics may bespeak a casual racism, but the music also reveals a deep and abiding love for the music, black and white, that made up the roots of rock 'n' roll. (And the Controllers' drummer, Karla "Mad Dog," was one of the few African Americans on the scene.)

As the hardcore style emerged, race itself was strangely almost absent. The social problems hardcore punks did address did not include race. If it is true, as one critic argues, that American hardcore was "the sound of whiteness under siege," a music that reflected an "underlying anxiety about race," this whiteness was neither acknowledged nor appreciated in Southern California.[3] Maybe that was because the great ethnic demographic transformation of Orange County did not begin until the late 1980s, or maybe it was because, despite the whiteness of the scene, Latinos held key positions in bands like Black Flag, Saccharine Trust, and Suicidal Tendencies, and one favorite hardcore venue was the Vex in East L.A. where the neighborhood (and the Samoan bouncers) disciplined the behavior of hardcore kids.[4]

Hardcore was also male music, at least initially, and at least in So Cal. Punk emerged immediately after the Women's Lib era as an important cultural site for girls and young women to play with identity.[5] In London and New York, singers and musicians like Poly Styrene, Siouxsie Sioux, Patti Smith, and Debbie Harry, in addition to the designer Vivienne Westwood, had played key roles in the development of punk. In Los Angeles, girls and young women at times seemed to dominate the scene, playing in bands, pogoing at the Masque, living at the Canterbury. With hardcore, however, girls and young women were pushed aside. Certainly, some still performed in bands, and many still went to shows. One of the first punk fans in all of Southern California, Lisa Fancher who wrote for Greg Shaw's *Bomp!* magazine in the mid-seventies, founded Frontier Records, which released important albums by the Circle Jerks, Adolescents, Suicidal Tendencies, and others.[6] But boys and young men dominated the scene in every way, especially physically, as the pit where the slamming occurred became a place where only the most fearless and physically fit dared to venture, and the rest of the audience was pushed to the edges.[7] While female voices did not disappear from the stage or the crowd, girls were more object than subject within hardcore. Many of the lyrics of hardcore bands testified to the teenage boy mentality, which saw girls as objects of lust, rage, and competition. The Adolescents, for example, managed to portray girls as simultaneously sluts and prudes in songs like "L.A. Girl" and "Creatures"—merely updating the traditional rock 'n' roll boys' position. Bands like the Angry Samoans and Fear relished explicit misogyny and homophobia, even as they claimed that it was all part of their joke-punk shtick.[8]

But hardcore was not the only game in town. Whether because of the violence or the limited nature of the artistic statement of hardcore, punk morphed into a variety of genres in the early 1980s. Many of the early punks stretched the boundaries of punk in different directions, exploring various mixtures with early rock 'n' roll and its forbears in R&B, blues, country, and even jazz. Some of the first proto-punks in L.A. had found their way to punk through their devotion to long-forgotten artists and genres, and they brought those passions to expanding punk's sound. The founder of the early zine *Back Door Man* founded the blues-punk band "Top Jimmy and the Rhythm Pigs." The Blasters, out of Downey, played homespun and gritty rockabilly. X incorporated elements of folk, country, and blues as they evolved. The Dils moved to San Francisco, then disbanded and moved to Austin, eventually forming the country rock band Rank and File. Robert Lopez of the Zeroes became El Vez, the Mexican Elvis.

Chris D., an early *Slash* contributor, continually remade his Flesh Eaters in order to explore different musical paths (and because it took him a few years to put his own band together). Their first album, with musicians from practically every Hollywood band contributing, was a frenetic slice of agitated junkie punk. The band on the second album consisted of members of the Blasters and X performing a haunting, voodoo-inspired swamp punk. After a couple of hard rock albums, Chris D. formed a new band, Divine Horseman—the name taken from Maya Deren's documentary on Haitian voodoo—singing country- and blues-tinged ballads. The only constants over the years were Chris D.'s Poe- and Rimbaud-inspired lyrics—"wonderful bleeding collages of B-movie dementia, street crime,

Mexican Catholicism and Dionysian punk spurt poetics"—and his unearthly howl—"powerful cat-scratched patterns of night-ripping fear, huge bursts of post-glottal raunch-vomit and cascades of pure and toxic love," in the words of punk writer and Flesh Eater devotee Byron Coley.[9]

Jeffrey Lee Pierce, another early *Slash* writer and Blondie Fan Club president, plundered the swamps to create his own howling punk-amped blues with an almost fetishistic devotion. Tito Larriva of the Plugz began to incorporate more Latin influences in his music and also fostered the development of a significant Chicano element in L.A. punk and hardcore, beginning with his support of Los Lobos (who would go on to record a hit with "La Bamba") in getting them booked as the opening act for Johnny Rotten's new band, Public Image Ltd., at the Olympic Auditorium in May 1980.[10] By 1982 a whole scene developed around the "Paisley Underground," a punk-tinged revival of sixties psychedelia led by the Dream Syndicate. Fans can claim that these bands produced the most important and lasting music out of the whole Southern California scene.

During the years of hardcore's ascendance in the suburbs, musicians in Los Angeles turned out an astounding variety of creative, new music, much of it roots-inspired. There was no clear divide between an urban and a suburban scene; it was all postsuburbia. The bands played all over the region, and fans crossed over from one genre to another. Even hardcore evolved, as Black Flag devolved into its Black Sabbath roots, the Minutemen churned out forty-song, forty-minute sets of their own peculiar polyglot, jazz-punk, and new bands like Saccharine Trust explored free-jazz-punk, the Descendents perfected popcore (long before Green Day), 45 Grave and Christian Death founded American goth, and so on. And these bands, scenes and subscenes cross-pollinated—through touring, records, and the proliferating zines—with an international postpunk musical subculture or set of subcultures that have continued the DIY tradition to this day. Back in England, Malcolm McLaren, the original manager of the Sex Pistols, had hooked up with Adam Ant to unleash the pirate-attired and spaghetti Western-themed Adam and the Ants on the British pop charts, while punk itself revived in league with the antiracism and antinuclear movements across Europe. The anarchist collective Crass, for example, confronted the Thatcherite assault on the welfare state and the revived Reaganite war machine with songs like "Do They Owe Us a Living?" and "Fight War, Not Wars."

Punk, hardcore, and postpunk scenes developed throughout the Western world. *Maximum Rocknroll*, the Bay Area zine, filed scene reports from across the United States and Europe, and even from behind the Iron Curtain. The scenes cohered around every conceivable variation of punk music and ideology, in every type of locale. While punk remained below the radar of the corporate record labels and mainstream rock radio, kids and young adults continued to gather to make and listen to punk-inspired music throughout the eighties.[11]

And then something happened in the rock music world that no one had predicted. In 1991 *Nevermind*, by the Olympia, Washington, punk band Nirvana, rocketed to the top of the pop charts, displacing Michael Jackson's comeback album *Dangerous*. Punk rock entered the mainstream. Throughout the eighties punk and its many variants had remained available as alternatives to rock fans coming of age. By the nineties, the vibrant underground scenes were producing music that the industry was finally able to market. Even if the industry behaved typically—scouring and hyping first Seattle and then any local scene they could find—and even if punks, in true punk fashion, complained that the music (by hit bands like Blink 182 and Good Charlotte) was watered down and commodified, many of the emerging bands paid homage to their forbears. Kurt Cobain of Nirvana gave credit whenever the opportunity arose to his role models in pathbreaking punk bands like the Wipers (the Portland band that had played at the Elks Lodge Massacre), the Meat Puppets (Arizonans who played with Nirvana on their legendary album *MTV Unplugged*), and the Germs. Indeed, one day in the summer of 1993, former Germs guitarist Pat Smear was manning the counter at the SST Record store on Sunset Boulevard when the phone rang. On the other end was Cobain, who invited Smear to join Nirvana for its upcoming tour. And thus, thirteen years after Darby Crash committed suicide and the Germs died with him, L.A. punk produced its first rock star.

But rock stardom was never the goal of L.A. punk and hardcore. Sure, there were some who saw the music as their path to fame and fortune. But since celebrity was highly unlikely, punks made the music for themselves. By the 1990s there was a critical mass of young people who had followed the underground scenes of the past decade—a kind of mass subculture. While hardcore had emerged in the postsuburban regions of Southern California, the area was not unique, as postsuburbia came to define the growing regions all around the country. Similarly, the rejection of mass culture and a universal youth culture that characterized L.A. punk was not unique, although other scenes developed different ideological emphases. The Bay Area scenes (Berkeley, San Francisco, San Jose, and other suburbs) generally promoted left-wing politics. In Washington, D.C., and its suburbs, punks created "straight edge" as bands like Minor Threat eschewed the sex and drugs normally associated with rock 'n' roll.

What united these scenes was the personal connection punks felt to their music and their scenes. Being a punk was more than a statement of fandom or musical preference. Punk was an identity. As D. Boon of the Minutemen sang in "History Lesson Part 2":

> We learned punk rock in Hollywood
> Drove up from [San] Pedro
> We were fucking corn dogs
> We'd go drink and pogo.

They were part of something larger than themselves, yet still separate from the mass. Punk scenes were communities, even if they were often fragmented and fragile. Through zines, bands, and touring, and sleeping on other punks' floors, punks created a dispersed, yet interconnected mass subculture. And they were no longer "fucking corn dogs."

Notes

Introduction

Epigraph: Kickboy Face, *Slash,* Vol. 3, No. 4 (1980), 30. The reference is to the recently overdosed Sid Vicious, bass player for England's most notorious punk band, the Sex Pistols.

1. Carducci, *Rock and the Pop Narcotic,* 369.
2. Heylin, *From the Velvets to the Voidoids,* 166–78.
3. Lawrence Grossberg calls these scenes "affective alliances" in *We Gotta Get Out of This Place.*

Chapter 1. "The Unheard Music"

1. Quoted in Morris, *Beyond and Back,* 11.
2. Quoted in ibid., 10.
3. Heylin, *From the Velvets to the Voidoids* and McNeil and McCain, *Please Kill Me.*
4. Burchill and Parsons, *"Boy Looked at Johnny,"* 3.
5. Marcus, *Lipstick Traces,* and Savage, *England's Dreaming.* For a critique of the idea that there is a link between punk and the Situationists, see Home, *Cranked Up Really High,* 19–30. Other important early works on punk include: Hebdige, *Subculture*; Frith, *Sound Effects*; and Laing, *One Chord Wonders.*
6. Kid Congo Powers in Spitz and Mullen, *We Got the Neutron Bomb,* 14.
7. For a nostalgic look at Rodney's, see Diana and Michelle, "Panic on the Strip," *Panic,* No. 1 (1978), 7–8. For a similar example from San Francisco, see Jennifer Miro's account of meeting Bowie at a party in Stark, *Punk '77.*
8. Stephen Davis, *Hammer of the Gods*; Cole and Trubo, *Stairway to Heaven*; and Spitz and Mullen, *We Got the Neutron Bomb.*
9. Ron Asheton in Spitz and Mullen, *We Got the Neutron Bomb,* 21.

10. This exchange comes from the transcription made by Zandra in *Generation X*, No. 2, 7. She also quotes David Bowie from the same television show as calling Iggy Pop's music "nihilistic rock."

11. Spitz and Mullen, *We Got the Neutron Bomb*, 54.

12. "Cliff Roman interview," *Spontaneous Combustion*, December 5, 2003, http://www.spontaneous.com/weirdos.html (accessed March 19, 2004).

13. Arnold, *Route 666*, 33.

14. For descriptions of this meeting and performance, see Spurrier, "Los Angeles Punk Rock," and Pleasant Gehman, "The Life of the Germs," *New York Rocker* (1982), reprinted in the liner notes to *(MIA): The Complete Anthology*. The quotation comes from Gehman.

15. *Time*, Vol. 110 (1977), 46–47.

16. Spurrier, "Los Angeles Punk Rock," 120.

17. Ibid., 119.

18. Lee, "Los Angeles," 11.

19. Spurrier, "Los Angeles Punk Rock," 119–20.

20. Lee, "Los Angeles," 11.

21. "Interview with Claude Bessy," *Maximum Rocknroll*, No. 127 (1994), n.p.

22. Lee, "Los Angeles," 11.

23. *Slash*, Vol. 1, No. 1 (1977), 3.

24. Lasch, *Culture of Narcissism*.

25. This is not to say that L.A. punk was not itself hedonistic. For an excellent account of disco, see Lawrence, *Love Saves the Day*.

26. An insightful look at American progressive rock is Mitchell Morris, "Kansas and the Prophetic Tone," *American Music* 18, No. 1 (Spring 2000): 1–38.

27. Quoted in Savage, *England's Dreaming*, 437.

28. Trudie Arguelles quoted in Spurrier, "Los Angeles Punk Rock," 121.

29. Lee, "Los Angeles," 11.

30. Ibid.

31. Mullen, liner notes to *Live from the Masque 1978*. But Mullen, nonetheless, closed the main entrance to the building because "idiots kept defacing" posters of movie stars like Mae West and Jean Harlow.

32. Ibid.

33. Ibid.

34. Ibid.

35. Ibid.

36. Ibid.

37. Spurrier, "Los Angeles Punk Rock," 121.

38. Cited in Gene Sculatti, "Everybody Needs Somebody to Hate," *Creem* (1981), 22.

39. Spurrier, "Los Angeles Punk Rock," 121.

40. D. D. Faye, quoted in *Los Angeles Times*, February 28, 1978, Section IV, p. 2.

41. Spurrier, "Los Angeles Punk Rock," 124.

42. For example, see the interview with Darby Crash in *Wasteland*, No. 3 (1978), 8: "I got art-damage. . . . Art damage is like you aren't supposed to smile in pictures"; and, *Generation X*, No. 5 (1978), 8: "All the groups in this town are art damaged."

43. Lee, "Los Angeles," 11.

44. Spurrier, "Los Angeles Punk Rock," 119.

45. Ibid.

46. *Slash*, Vol. 1, No. 9 (1978), 4.

47. Lee, "Los Angeles," 22.

48. Spurrier, "Los Angeles Punk Rock," 121.

49. Quoted in Spurrier, "Los Angeles Punk Rock," 120.

50. Thornton, *Club Cultures*, 10.

51. Lee, "Los Angeles," 17.

52. Frith, *Sound Effects*, 11.

53. Shank, *Dissonant Identities*.

54. Thornton, *Club Cultures*, 26.

55. Ibid., 30.

Chapter 2. "Destroy All Music"

1. Belsito and Davis, *Hardcore California*, 21.

2. For Meltzer as emcee at the Sex Pistols show, see Monk and Guterman, *12 Days on the Road*, 218–19; and Meltzer, *Whore Just Like the Rest*, 281.

3. Greil Marcus, quoted in Savage, *England's Dreaming*, 458.

4. *The Great Rock 'n' roll Swindle* is the name of the McLaren-inspired film of the Sex Pistols' history.

5. Belsito and Davis, *Hardcore California*, 21; Savage, *England's Dreaming*, 458; and Monk and Guterman, *12 Days on the Road*, 225–28. Other accounts have Sid being resuscitated by the Haight Ashbury Free Clinic: Spitz and Mullen, *We Got the Neutron Bomb*, 156; Lydon and Zimmerman, *Rotten*, 237–52.

6. McNeil and McCain, *Please Kill Me*.

7. Quoted in Savage, *England's Dreaming*, 460. See also his article for *Punk*, No. 14 (1978), 47: "The concert sucks. Johnny Rotten is boring. The sound is horrible. I have a feeling Bill Graham fucked up the sound on purpose."

8. Belsito and Davis, *Hardcore California*, 22.

9. See quotes from members of the Nuns and Avengers in Stark, *Punk '77*, 41–43, and *Search and Destroy*, No. 6 (1978), 13. Danny Furious, Avengers' drummer, is quoted in Peter Belsito's essay on San Francisco punk in Belsito and Davis, *Hardcore California*, 77.

10. Quoted in Savage, *England's Dreaming*, 457–58.

11. Penelope Houston in Stark and Mullen, *We Got the Neutron Bomb*, 155.

12. Pat Ryan, the bass player for the Nuns, in Stark, *Punk '77*, 41–42.

13. Stephen Zepeda, *The L.A. Beat*, No. 1 (1978), 17.

14. Randy and Pleasant, "Sex Pistols at Winterland, San Francisco," *Lobotomy*, Vol. 1,

No. 3 (1978), n.p.

15. Kickboy Face, "Other People's Misery," *Slash*, Vol. 1, No. 8 (1978), 18–21. On page 24 of the same issue Bird Protractor refers to the show as "rather disappointing."

16. Arnold, *Route 666*, 3.

17. Ibid.

18. Stansell, *City of Women*, 91–95.

19. Kett, *Rites of Passage*.

20. Nasaw, *Children of the City*, 196.

21. For Bourne on the standardization of American culture, see Bourne, "Transnational America." For his hope that youth would become a progressive force in American society, see his essays opposing U.S. involvement in World War I: "Below the Battle," "A War Diary," and "Twilight of Idols," in *Untimely Papers*. See also *Youth and Life*. See also Addams, *Spirit of Youth*.

22. Youth culture fads, Paula Fass writes, bound the young to the realities of the society—epitomizing the rapid pace of change, making constant adjustment necessary, and symbolizing the new ethic of consumption. Fads were one effective way in which the needs of the young were being channeled into the historical conditions of a changing society. Fass, *The Damned and the Beautiful*, 227–28. See also Allen, *Only Yesterday*, for the fads of the twenties.

23. Lynd and Lynd, *Middletown*.

24. See, for example, Blumer, *Movies and Conduct*, and W. W. Charters, *Motion Pictures*.

25. Tocqueville, *Democracy in America*, see especially "In What Spirit the Americans Cultivate the Arts," 169–73; Horkheimer and Adorno, "The Culture Industry: Enlightenment as Mass Deception," in *Dialectic of Enlightenment*, 120–67; Macdonald, "Theory of Mass Culture," 71. Also collected in Rosenberg and White, *Mass Culture*, are important articles by Clement Greenberg, Irving Howe, Leslie Fiedler, Bernard Rosenberg, David White, José Ortega y Gasset, Leo Lowenthal, Gilbert Seldes, David Reisman, Marshall McLuhan, and many others. The anti-mass culture arguments mirror the contemporary and influential critiques of conformist America in Riesman, *Lonely Crowd*, and Mills, *White Collar*. Also very influential was Lowenthal, "Triumph of Mass Idols." See also, Rosenberg and White, *Mass Culture Revisited*.

26. See Gilbert, *Cycle of Outrage*, and Rosenberg and White, *Mass Culture*.

27. Gilbert argues that the moral panic resulted from a misunderstanding on the part of adults of large-scale social transformations occurring in the United States: "If indeed it was partly a symbolic term, delinquency represented a projection of uneasiness, a measure of discomfort that adults felt about the social and cultural changes that touched them too. . . . Youth more than adults bore the imprint of these changes. They were the harbingers of a new society, and adults were prepared to punish the messengers so much did they wish to avoid the message that the family was rapidly changing, that affluence was undercutting old mores, that working women were altering the sexual politics of the home and workplace, and that the media were transforming American culture into a homogenized mass that disguised local distinctions

and prepared the way for a new sort of social order" (Gilbert, *Cycle of Outrage*, 41). See also Engelhardt, *End of Victory Culture*, especially 133–54.

28. See Gabler, *Empire of Their Own*, and "Against the Wind: Dialogic Aspects of Rock and Roll" in Lipsitz, *Time Passages*, 99–132.

29. See "The Meaning of Memory: Family, Class, and Ethnicity in Early Network Television," and "Why Remember Mama? The Changing Face of a Women's Narrative," in Lipsitz, *Time Passages*, 39–98; Miller, "Prime Time"; and "Television in the Family Circle" in Spigel, *Make Room for TV*, 36–72.

30. Gilbert, *Cycle of Outrage*, 195.

31. Breines, *Young, White and Miserable*, 151, 154.

32. Douglas, *Where the Girls Are*, 87.

33. Gitlin, *The Sixties*, 197.

34. See Frank, *Conquest of Cool*, 29. I do not mean to oversimplify the history of the sixties or of youth culture, but to draw out the specific point about the relationship between youth culture and mass culture.

35. See Harvey, *Condition of Postmodernity*.

36. As Landon Y. Jones puts it, "In the 1970s, the single fastest-growing age group was 25–34, the family building years beloved by merchandisers for their heavy-spending habits" (Jones, *Great Expectations*, 218).

37. Kett, *Rites of Passage*, 266, 272.

38. Postman, *Disappearance of Childhood*.

39. The sociologist Ralph Larkin argues that "adolescence" ended with the arrival of postscarcity society and monopoly capitalism: "Almost as theories of adolescence were being formulated, they were being undermined. Most of the writers on adolescence appeared in the 1950s. Yet Gillis (1974), writing in the 1970s, sees adolescence as ending in the 1950s. Edgar Friedenberg heralded the end of adolescence in 1959. The silent generation of the 1950s with its isolated 'rebel without a cause' signaled the end of the adolescent struggle for an autonomous identity" (Larkin, *Suburban Youth in Cultural Crisis*, 42). Larkin actually argues that "youth" replaces "adolescence" with postscarcity society and monopoly capitalism, but he apparently sees youth as no more than an age group, unrelated to any psychological development.

40. Peterson and Berger, "Cycles in Symbol Production," 154. See also: Friedlander, *Rock and Roll*; Goodman, *Mansion on a Hill*; and Dannen, *Hit Men*.

41. Peterson and Berger, "Cycles in Symbol Production," 154.

42. Frith, "'The magic that can set you free,'" 159–68.

43. Duncombe, *Notes from Underground*, 117.

44. Interview with Falling James.

45. "Bomp Records: Twenty Years of Keeping Rock'n'Roll Alive," *Goldmine*, Vol. 21, No. 10 (1995), 56.

46. Quoted in ibid., 56.

47. "Greg Shaw Interview," *Panic*, No. 1 (1978), 21.

48. "Greg Shaw," *Flipside*, No. 89 (1994), n.p.

49. Ibid., 89.

50. Lisa Fancher, letter to the editor, *Rockin' in the Fourth Estate*, No. 2 (Spring 1979), 3. Fancher would go on to found Frontier Records, an important hardcore punk label.

51. *Panic*, No. 1 (1978), 21.

52. *Flipside*, No. 89 (1994). Shaw claimed Sky Dog in France was the first in the world, and he believed that Bomp was the model for Stiff Records, the first independent in England.

53. See McKenna, "Burned Bridges."

54. "Interview with Dave Trout" of The Weirdos, *Flipside*, No. 4 (1977), n.p.

55. The song was "surreptitiously recorded at an abortive casting call for Cheech and Chong's Up in Smoke" (Morris, "Darby Crash," 44).

56. *Flipside*, No. 1 (1977), n.p.

57. "Interview with Rodney," *Flipside,* No. 5 (1977), n.p.

Chapter 3. "Message from the Underground"

1. The bands performing on the nights of February 24 and 25, 1978 were the Zeros, Eyes, Screamers, Germs, Controllers, Bags, Deadbeats, Weirdos, Dickies, Shock, Skulls, Alley Cats, Black Randy, F-Word, Flesh Eaters, Plugz, and X.

2. The phrase "synth hysteria" is from Savage, *England's Dreaming*, 584.

3. *Los Angeles Times*, February 27, 1978, sec. IV.

4. Ibid., February 28, 1978, sec. IV.

5. Ibid., Sept 27, 1977, sec. IV.

6. Ibid., February 28, 1978, sec. IV.

7. *Slash*, Vol. 1, No. 9 (1978), 18.

8. Ibid., 24.

9. Marcus, *Lipstick Traces*.

10. Ibid., 18.

11. Philomena Winstanley, "Interview with Claude Bessy," *Maximum Rocknroll*, No. 127 (1993), n.p.

12. Quoted in Jeff Spurrier, "Los Angeles Punk Rock," 120.

13. *Slash*, Vol. 1, No. 10 (1978), 6.

14. For examples see *Bomp!* Vol. 3, No. 7 (1976–77), 40–41, and Vol. 4, No. 1 (Nov. 1977).

15. *Slash*, Vol. 1, No. 7 (1978), 20.

16. El-Tot sira, letter to *Slash*, Vol. 1, No. 8 (1978), 10.

17. Brendan Mullen, letter to *Slash*, Vol. 1, No. 10 (1978), 6.

18. Shaw had written in his earlier letter to *Slash*: "It was me or Mark [Shipper] who actually coined the phrase 'punk rock.' Did you know that? In 1971!" *Slash*, Vol. 1, No. 2 (1977), n.p.

19. See Pooch, "Rocking before the Masque," *Flipside*, No. 54 (1986), 6.

20. *Slash*, Vol. 1, No. 9 (1978), 8.

21. Kickboy Face, response to letter from Richard Humbert, *Slash*, Vol. 1, No. 8

(1978), 10; Editorial, *Slash*, Vol. 1, No. 5 (1977), 3.

22. See also the special issue of Shaw's *Bomp!* on power pop: *Bomp!* No. 18 (1978).

23. See Hoskyns, *Waiting for the Sun*.

24. *Slash*, Vol. 1, No. 9 (1978), 20.

25. M. Saunders, T. Homer, G. Turner, "Get Off the Air," Haizman Music, BMI (1980), on The Angry Samoans, *Inside My Brain*.

26. Morris, *Beyond and Back*, 22.

27. Interview with Stephen Shea.

28. *Slash*, Vol. 1, No. 10 (1978), 4.

29. For Meltzer's account of his involvement with punk, see Meltzer, *L.A. is the Capital of Kansas*, 143–45.

30. See the ads on the pages of any issue of *Slash*.

31. See "The Trashing of the Troubadour," *Slash* Vol. 1, No. 9 (1978), 21.

32. See Gillett, *Sound of the City*, and Frith, *Sound Effects*.

33. Gorilla, "Snipes," *Slash*, Vol. 1, No. 9 (1978), 6.

34. See "Canterbury Tales," *Slash* (1978), and Belsito and Davis, *Hardcore California*.

35. Craig Lee, "Hollywood's Bad Habit," *New York Rocker* (1981), and Spurrier, "Los Angeles Punk Rock."

36. *Slash*, Vol. 3, No. 3 (1980), 5.

37. Eliot, *Rockonomics*, 187.

38. Hoskyns, *Waiting for the Sun*, 297. For a nice tribute to the drummer whose beat defined the song, see John Kelly, "Bruce Gary and the Riff He Drummed Into Your Head," *Washington Post*, August 25, 2006, C01.

39. See *Los Angeles Times* series on "L.A.'s Rock Renaissance," which ran from June to August of 1980 and covered almost exclusively the poppier New Wave acts; see also the following issues of *Record Review*: Vol. 3, No. 5 (1979); Vol. 3, No. 6 (1979); Vol. 4, No. 1 (1980); Vol. 4, No. 2 (1980); and Vol. 4, No. 3 (1980). And see Chris Morris, "L.A.'s Rock & Roll Renaissance," *Rolling Stone,* Vol. 321 (July 10, 1980), 12–14, which focuses on the New Wave bands but mentions how the major labels ignored punk bands like the Plugz, the Germs, and X.

40. The account of The Damned show comes from my own memories. No, I was not that kid, but I spoke with him before the second set, getting his account of his thrashing. I witnessed Rat Scabies hitting someone—not his intended target, by the way—in the head with the guitar.

Chapter 4. "Damaged"

1. Jeffrey Shore, "Bouncing at the Whiskey," in Eisen, Fine, and Eisen, *Unknown California*, 379. The article first appeared in the *L.A. Weekly* in 1981.

2. Geza X, liner notes to Germs, *Rock N' Rule*.

3. For a moving account of the life of Darby Crash, see Mullen, Bolles, and Parfrey, *Lexicon Devil*.

4. Hebdige, *Subculture*, 132.

5. Frith, *Sound Effects*, 158.

6. Fogelson, *Fragmented Metropolis*; Fishman, *Bourgeois Utopias*, chapter 6.

7. Soja, "Los Angeles, 1965–1992," in Scott and Soja, *Los Angeles and Urban Theory*, 426.

8. Water was—and is—a continual problem. Beginning in the first years of the twentieth century, civic and business leaders concocted plans to build aqueducts to siphon off water from the Owens River and, later, the Colorado River. See Reisner, *Cadillac Desert*.

9. Jackson, *Crabgrass Frontier*, 122.

10. Fogelson, *Fragmented Metropolis*, chapter 5. Fogelson says that the population of L.A. "quadrupled in the 1880's, doubled in the 1890's, tripled in the 1900's, and doubled in the 1910's and again in the 1920's" (78).

11. Ibid., 105.

12. Jackson, *Crabgrass Frontier*, 178–79. See also, Fred W. Viehe, "Black Gold Suburbs: The Influence of the Extractive Industry on the Suburbanization of Los Angeles," *Journal of Urban History* 8 (November 1981): 3–26.

13. Viehe, "Black Gold Suburbs," and Jackson, *Crabgrass Frontier*, 179.

14. Jackson, *Crabgrass Frontier*, 179.

15. Fishman, *Bourgeois Utopias*, 167–72. See also Fogelson, *Fragmented Metropolis*, chapter 8, and, especially, Bottles, *Los Angeles and the Automobile*. An excellent recent summary of the link between transportation policy and political power is Wachs, "Evolution of Transportation Policy."

16. Fishman, *Bourgeois Utopias*, 179.

17. See Kasarda, "Urbanization, Community, and the Metropolitan Problem"; Gottdiener, "Social Planning and Metropolitan Growth"; Rowe, *Making a Middle Landscape*; and Findlay, "Stanford Industrial Park: Downtown for Silicon Valley," in *Magic Lands*, 117–59.

18. Jackson, *Crabgrass Frontier*. On page ix, Jackson credits Richard C. Wade with coining the term.

19. Kasarda, "Urbanization, Community, and the Metropolitan Problem," 34, and Baldassare, *Cities and Urban Living*, 12.

20. See, for example, Nicolaides, *My Blue Heaven*, and McGirr, *Suburban Warriors*.

21. Jackson, *Crabgrass Frontier*, 287.

22. See Josh Sides, "Straight into Compton: American Dreams, Urban Nightmares, and the Metamorphosis of a Black Suburb," *American Quarterly*, Vol. 56, No. 3 (2004). Edward Soja argues that the Watts rebellion and other urban uprisings of the late 1960s "marked one of the beginnings of the end of the postwar economic boom and the social contract and Fordist/Keynesian state planning that underpinned its propulsiveness" (*The City*, 431). The connection between the local development of postsuburbia and national and international political and economic transformations will be explored later in this chapter.

23. Teaford, *Post-Suburbia*, 53, 59, and all of chapter 3.

24. Abbott, *Metropolitan Frontier*, 61.

25. Harvey, *Condition of Postmodernity*, 145.

26. Abbott, *Metropolitan Frontier*, 77.

27. Interview with Pooch.

28. Ray Cook, "Middle Class," *Damage*, No. 12–13 (1981), 56.

29. "Middle Class [interview by Howard Etc.]," *Forget It!* No. 6 (ca. 1980), 5. In Belsito and Davis, *Hardcore California*, 30, Craig Lee identifies the date as August 1978, but his dates are not reliable.

30. *Slash*, Vol. 1, No. 11 (1978), 28.

31. Review of Lobotomy at the Whisky, ibid., 25. No author is cited for this review, but parts are excerpted in the liner notes to the Middle Class collection *a blueprint for joy 1978–1980* and attributed to David Wiley. See also, Review of Canterbury Night at the Rock Corporation, *Slash*, Vol. 2, No. 1 (1978), 18.

32. Review of the Dickies and the Middle Class at the Whisky, *Slash*, Vol. 2, No. 1 (1978), 19.

33. Middle Class, *Out of Vogue* (Joke Records, 1978). For more on the Middle Class as in between the Hollywood and beach scenes, see "Middle Class [interview by Howard Etc.]," *Forget It!* No. 6 (ca. 1980), 5–11.

34. Spot, liner notes to *Everything Went Black*.

35. Tim Tonooka, Interview with Black Flag, *Ripper*, No. 3 (ca. 1980), 15.

36. Spot, liner notes to *Everything Went Black*.

37. *Slash*, Vol 2, No. 10 (1979), 14.

38. "The Church," *Flipside*, No. 17 (1979), n.p.

39. *Slash*, Vol. 2, No. 10 (1979), 13.

40. Carducci, *Rock and the Pop Narcotic*, 369.

41. *Slash*, Vol. 2, No. 9 (1979), 14.

42. Pavitt, liner notes to *American Youth Report*.

43. Offer, Ostrov, and Howard, *Adolescent*, 102. A sociological study of Orange County, California, in the early 1980s found that "mental health ratings" were poorest for those in the 18–24 age group; Baldassare, *Trouble in Paradise*, 13–14.

44. Cote and Allahar, *Generation on Hold*, xvii, 68.

45. Larkin, *Suburban Youth in Cultural Crisis*, 145.46. Cote and Allahar, *Generation on Hold*, 22.

47. Venkatesh, "Changing Consumption Patterns," 153.

48. Cameron Crowe, *Fast Times at Ridgemont High* (Universal Pictures, 1982).

49. Fishman, *Bourgeois Utopias*, 185. Fishman shows how there were signs of this development in Los Angeles as early as the 1920s, 172.

50. Jackson, *Crabgrass Frontier*, 279.

51. Davis, *City of Quartz*, chapter 4; Jackson, *Crabgrass Frontier*, 301.

52. Liner notes to *Someone's Gonna Get Their Head*. See also liner notes to *Someone Got Their Head Kicked In!* and *Generation Magazine*, Vol. 1, No. 1 (1983).

53. Boehm, "Kids of the Black Hole."

54. Kalefa Sanneh, *New York Times*, September 21, 2006, makes a similar point.

55. Poster, "Narcissism or Liberation." See also, Long and Glick, "Family Patterns in

Suburban Areas," and Wilson, "Family in Suburbia."

56. Interviews with Matt Bokovoy and Tony Reflex (July 12, 1995); and Boehm, "Kids of the Black Hole."

57. Descendents, "Suburban Home," on *Milo Goes to College* (SST Records, 1982).

Chapter 5. "Brats in Battalions"

1. Interview with Tito Larriva; *Slash*, Vol. 1, No. 10 (1978), p. 18.

2. Mullen, liner notes to *Live from the Masque 1978.*

3. Review of the Middle Class, Negative Trend, Weirdos, and Dils at the Azteca, *Slash*, Vol. 2, No. 1 (1978), 19.

4. Interview with Pooch.

5. See the indispensable doctoral dissertation by David McBride, "On the Fault Line of Mass Culture and Counterculture: A Social History of the Hippie Counterculture in 1960s Los Angeles" (UCLA, 1998).

6. The events at the Elks Lodge are reconstructed from my own memories; interview with Stephen Shea; interview with Katie Golden; interview with Raymond Bridgers; interview with Tito Larriva; Spurrier, "Los Angeles Punk Rock"; Interview with Claude Bessy and Philomena Winstanley, *Maximum Rocknroll*, No. 127; Craig Lee in Belsito and Davis, *Hardcore California.*

7. Barry Shank describes a similar event in the Austin, Texas, scene in Shank, *Dissonant Identities.*

8. Interview with Black Flag, *Forget It!* No. 6 (ca. 1980), 21.

9. See Chris Martin, "Nobody Got Famous in H.B.," *Flipside*, No. 92 (1994), n.p.; Adolescents interview on KNAC Radio; Interview with Eddie Subtitle, *Slash*, Vol. 2, No. 10 (1979), 13.

10. Patrick Goldstein, *Los Angeles Times*, June 29, 1980, Calendar section. Meanwhile, only a week before the *Times* had presented X as one of the best of the year; compared to hardcore, punk now seemed respectable and mainstream. See *Los Angeles Times*, June 22, 1980, Calendar section, and April 29, 1980, sec. VI.

11. For more on the U.S. media portrayal of punk, see MacLeod, "'Social Distortion.'"

12. *Class of 1984* (United Film Distribution, 1982); *Road Warrior* (Warner Bros. Pictures, 1982); *Return of the Living Dead* (Orion Pictures, 1985); *Suburbia* (New World Pictures, 1984); *Repo Man* (Universal Pictures, 1984); *CHiPs*, "Battle of the Bands"; *Quincy, M.E.*, "Next Stop, Nowhere"; *Donahue*, "Parents of Punkers"; *Jughead*, No. 327 (1983); *People*, Vol. 19 (1983), 96–97; *Hunter*, "Death Machine."

13. See interview with Black Flag by Tim Tonooka in *Ripper*, No. 3 (1980), 15, and Editorial, *Flipside*, No. 19 (1980), n.p.

14. Editorial, *Flipside*, No. 19 (1980), n.p.

15. Shreader in Belsito and Davis, *Hardcore California*, 47–48.

16. The major forces behind the politicization of punk in Northern California were the people associated with the radio show and zine *Maximum Rocknroll*, but

punk culture in general in the area was conducive to a leftist version of anarchism, especially in the East Bay scene centered in Berkeley. See Goldthorpe, "Intoxicated Culture," and Duncombe, *Notes from Underground*, especially chapter 8.

17. Certeau, *Practice of Everyday Life*; Lefebvre, *Everyday Life in the Modern World*; Lefebvre, *Critique of Everyday Life*; Blanchot, "Everyday Speech," 12–20; and Holt, "Marking," 1–20.

18. Soja, "Inside Exopolis," 121.

19. See Schiesl, "Designing the Model Community," 55–91.

20. Soja, "Inside Exopolis," 116–17.

21. Certeau, *Practice of Everyday Life*, 96.

22. Certeau, *Practice of Everyday Life*, xvii. In part, Certeau's notion of everyday life follows Michel Foucault, who attempted to trace the "microphysics of power," that is the establishment of discipline in all its details. But Foucault still privileges the productive apparatus, underestimating the ability of people to not only resist, but shape the development of power. That is, Foucault leaves no room for people to act as agents. Certeau's everyday life, on the other hand, concentrates on exploring those "multiform, resistan[t], tricky and stubborn procedures that elude discipline without being outside the field in which it is exercised."

23. Certeau, *Practice of Everyday Life*, xii.

24. Lefebvre, *Everyday Life in the Modern World*, 91.

25. Certeau, *Practice of Everyday Life*, ix.

26. Hebdige, *Subculture*.

27. Interview with Jon Lalanne.

28. Incidentally, this dovetailed in interesting ways with another dominant 1980s motif, Reaganomics. The punk influence on surfing brought in a revolution in design, with boards having wild patterns and bright colors; wet suits were for the first time not basic black but multicolored and dayglo; and surfing surged forward as a big business, with influence on national fashions and merchandising (as it had a couple of times before in the postwar era) but also as a competitive sport with major corporate sponsors and large money tournaments. Punk surfers also heightened the territorialism of surf culture, a feature which was already existent and intensified with the increased popularity of surfing in the early eighties.

29. Matt Bokovoy clued me in to this aspect of skate punk culture. See the excellent article by Willard, "Seance, Tricknowlogy." In the early eighties the skateboarding magazine *Thrasher* began to feature interviews with hardcore punk bands. Listen, also, to the Adolescents' "Skate Babylon" on *Brats in Battalions* (Triple X, 1987).

30. The Starwood and Whisky in Hollywood changed their policies on booking punk seemingly every month. The Costa Mesa community board eventually succeeded in closing down the punk club the Cuckoo's Nest for good after the case had gone to the state supreme court. Joe Vex ran "the Vex" in no fewer than three locations, being shut down continually by the fire and police departments. See *Flipside*, No. 24 (1981), n.p.

31. Adolescents interview on KNAC Radio.

32. Battalion of Saints, "Cops are Out," on Various Artists, *Someone's Gonna Get Their Head to Believe in Something* (Better Youth Organization, 1992).

33. Interview with Blaze James.

34. Davis, *City of Quartz*, 101.

35. Lamb, *As Orange Goes*, 3–5. Lamb points out that in 1968 there were three thousand members of the John Birch Society in Orange County out of a population of 1.3 million, a percentage which does not fit with the contemporary public image of the people in Orange County as rabid Birchers (14). For a brilliant history of the origins in Southern California of the national conservative politics of the 1980s, see McGirr, *Suburban Warriors*.

36. "Roughly since the beginning of the Kennedy-Johnson boom homeowner politics have focused on defense of the suburban dream against unwanted development (industry, apartments and offices) as well as against unwanted persons" (Davis, *City of Quartz*, 170).

37. Danielson, *Politics of Exclusion*.

38. As David Clark writes, "Housing demand increased as the baby boom generation matured and formed new households, and migration to the area resumed when the aerospace industry came out of its early 1970s slump. In 1970 the average Southern California home sold at the national medium price of $32,000. By mid-1981 the average U.S. home price came to $74,000, but in the Los Angeles five-county area the figure had shot up to $118,000. Skyrocketing prices led to sky-high tax assessments" (Clark, "Improbable Los Angeles," 296).

39. Lo, *Small Property versus Big Government*, 11, 10.

40. Ibid., 42, 72.

41. Davis, *City of Quartz*, 156.

42. Ibid., 180.

43. Lo, *Small Property versus Big Government*; the quote comes from Clark, "Improbable Los Angeles," to describe the "motto of Southern California politics as the 1980s opened" (297).

44. Davis, *City of Quartz*, 181; Lo, *Small Property versus Big Government*.

45. See *Flipside*, No. 20 (1980), and *Damage*, No. 11 (1980). See also *Outcry*, No. 1 (ca. 1981).

46. Brendan Mullen, "L.A.," *Damage*, No. 11 (1980), 33.

47. Jonathan Formula, "Welcome to the War Zone: The Suburbs Strike Back," *Damage*, No. 11 (1980), 42.

48. Ibid., 42.

49. Chris Martin, "Nobody Got Famous in H.B.," *Flipside*, No. 92 (1994), n.p.

50. "The Joykiller," *Flipside*, No. 100 (1996), n.p.

51. Jeffrey Bale, "Black Flag: Soundtrack for Armageddon," *Damage*, No. 11 (1980), 11.

52. I don't mean to set up an invidious distinction here, with Hollywood punks more properly "political" in their philosophy. Clearly, the Masque scene was as much about having fun and getting wasted as about rebellion.

53. Martin, "Nobody Got Famous in H.B."

54. Ibid.

55. Jonathan Formula, "Introduction," to Belsito and Davis, *Hardcore California*, 5.

56. See Spot, liner notes to *Everything Went Black*.

57. *Flipside*, No. 24 (1981), n.p.

58. Ibid.

59. *Outcry*, No. 3 (1982), n.p.

60. Interview with Tony Reflex, May 10, 1997.

61. Rollins, *Get in the Van*, 110–11.

62. Also interview with Tony Reflex, October 3, 1995.

63. Azzerad, *Our Band Could Be Your Life*, 74. His chapters on Black Flag and the Minutemen are wonderful, if a bit hagiographic. See also Tim Irwin, *We Jam Econo: The Story of the Minutemen* (Rocket Fuel Films, 2005), a fine documentary.

64. Rollins, *Get in the Van*, 11, 14.

65. Interview in *Decline of Western Civilization* and Tim Tonooka, "Black Flag," *Ripper*, No. 3 (ca. 1980), 12–18.

66. See Mike Watt in *Musician*, No. 199 (1995), 30, 49–50; and, interview with Black Flag in *Ripper*, No. 3 (ca. 1980), 12–18.

67. Interview with Black Flag, *Ripper*, No. 3 (ca. 1980), 16.

68. Ibid.

69. Quoted in *BAM*, No. 162 (1983), 30.

70. See Spot, liner notes to *Everything Went Black*.

71. *BAM*, No. 99 (1981), 14–16.

Conclusion: "Punk Rock Changed Our Lives"

1. For a beautifully written and chilling account of neo-Nazi skinheads in the Antelope Valley (in the inland desert area of Southern California) in the 1990s, see Finnegan, *Cold New World*, 269–340.

2. See Eric Lott, *Love and Theft: Blackface Minstrelsy and the American Working Class* (1995).

3. Kelefa Sanneh, "How Hard Was Their Core? Looking Back at Anger," *New York Times*, September 21, 2006, E1.

4. A good source for the demographic changes in this era is Waldinger and Bozorg-mehr, *Ethnic Los Angeles*.

5. See Douglas, *Where the Girls Are*; Reynolds and Press, *Sex Revolts*; and McRobbie, *Postmodernism and Popular Culture*.

6. For one example of her early writing see Fancher, "Are You Young and Rebellious?" The article was originally published in *Who Put the Bomp!* (Spring 1976).

7. Leslie G. Roman, in "Intimacy, Labor, and Class," explores how girls' and young women's subjectivities developed along the edges in her sociological study of female punks in a Midwestern city in the early eighties.

8. By the mid-eighties, *Maximum Rocknroll* in the Bay Area—always more explic-

itly political than any zine from the Southern California scene—began to explore the position of women in punk and address feminism directly. Their work became a direct influence on the Riot Grrl movement of the early nineties. For Riot Grrls, see Gottlieb and Wald, "Smells Like Teen Spirit."

9. Coley, liner notes to *No Questions Asked*.

10. Interview with Tito Larriva. Lipsitz's otherwise excellent and important article, "Cruising Around the Historical Bloc: Postmodernism and Popular Music in East Los Angeles" in *Time Passages*, unfortunately misses the influence of the Plugz altogether.

11. See Arnold, *Route 666*, and Azzerad, *Our Band Could Be Your Life*, for chronicles of the eighties underground music scenes. For fun and informative, if disjointed, accounts of the evolution of punk and hardcore, see Blush, *American Hardcore*.

Bibliography

Punk Memoirs and Commentary

The Adolescents. Interview on KNAC Radio, October 12, 1981. Audiotape of interview is in possession of Tony Reflex.

Arnold, Gina. *Route 666: On the Road to Nirvana.* New York: St. Martin's, 1993.

Belsito, Peter, and Bob Davis, eds. *Hardcore California: A History of Punk and New Wave.* San Francisco: Last Gasp, 1983.

Blush, Stephen. *American Hardcore: A Tribal History.* Los Angeles: Feral House, 2006.

Boehm, Mike. "Kids of the Black Hole." *Los Angeles Times,* July 23, 1989, Calendar Section.

Burchill, Julie, and Tony Parsons. *"The Boy Looked at Johnny": The Obituary of Rock and Roll.* 1978. Reprint, Boston: Faber and Faber, 1987.

Carducci, Joe. *Rock and the Pop Narcotic: Testament for the Electric Church.* 2nd rev. ed. Los Angeles: 2.13.61, 1994.

Fancher, Lisa. "Are You Young and Rebellious Enough to Love the Runaways?" In *Rock She Wrote: Women Write about Rock, Pop, and Rap,* edited by Evelyn McDonnell and Ann Powers, 285–90. New York: Cooper Square, 1995.

Goldthorpe, Jeff. "Intoxicated Culture: Punk Symbolism and Punk Protest." *Socialist Review* 22, no. 2 (April–June 1992): 35–64.

Hebdige, Dick. *Subculture: The Meaning of Style.* London: Routledge, 1979.

Henry, Tricia. *Break All Rules! Punk Rock and the Making of a Style.* Ann Arbor, Mich.: UMI Research Press, 1989.

Heylin, Clinton. *From the Velvets to the Voidoids: A Pre-Punk History for a Post-Punk World.* New York: Penguin, 1993.

Home, Stewart. *Cranked Up Really High: Genre Theory and Punk Rock.* Hove, UK: CodeX, 1995.

Laing, David. *One Chord Wonders: Power and Meaning in Punk Rock.* Milton Keynes, UK: Open University Press, 1985.

Lee, Craig, "Los Angeles." In *Hardcore California: A History of Punk and New Wave,* edited by Peter Belsito and Bob Davis, 10–40. San Francisco: Last Gasp, 1983.

Lydon, John, and Keith Zimmerman. *Rotten: No Irish, No Blacks, No Dogs.* New York: St. Martin's, 1993.

MacLeod, Dewar. "'Social Distortion': The Rise of Suburban Punk Rock in Los Angeles." In *America under Construction: Boundaries and Identities in Popular Culture,* edited by Kristi S. Long and Matthew Nadelhaft, 123–48. New York: Garland, 1997.

McKenna, Kristine. "Burned Bridges & Vials of Blood." In *Make the Music Go Bang: The Early L.A. Punk Scene,* edited by Don Snowden, 39–45. New York: St. Martin's, 1997.

McNeil, Legs, and Gillian McCain. *Please Kill Me: The Uncensored Oral History of Punk.* New York: Penguin, 1997.

Monk, Noel E., and Jimmy Guterman. *12 Days on the Road: The Sex Pistols and America.* New York: Harper Collins, 1990.

Morris, Chris. *Beyond and Back: The Story of X.* San Francisco: Last Gasp, 1983.

———. "Darby Crash: The American Sid Vicious." *Request,* August 1995, 40–44, 72–73.

Mullen, Brendan, Don Bolles, and Adam Parfrey. *Lexicon Devil: The Fast Times and Short Life of Darby Crash and the Germs.* Los Angeles: Feral House, 2002.

Rollins, Henry. *Get in the Van: On the Road with Black Flag.* Los Angeles: 2.13.61, 1994.

Roman, Leslie G. "Intimacy, Labor, and Class: Ideologies of Feminine Sexuality in the Punk Slam Dance." In *Becoming Feminine: The Politics of Popular Culture*, edited by Leslie G. Roman and Linda K. Christian-Smith, 143–84. New York: Falmer, 1988.

Savage, Jon. *England's Dreaming: Anarchy, Sex Pistols, Punk Rock, and Beyond.* New York: St. Martin's, 1992.

Spitz, Mark, and Brendan Mullen. *We Got the Neutron Bomb: The Untold Story of L.A. Punk.* New York: Three Rivers Press, 2001.

Spurrier, Jeff. "Los Angeles Punk Rock." *Details,* December 1994, 119–21.

Stark, James. *Punk '77: An Inside Look at the San Francisco Rock n' Roll Scene, 1977.* San Francisco: Stark Grafix, 1992.

Books and Articles

Abbott, Carl. *The Metropolitan Frontier: Cities in the Modern American West.* Tucson: University of Arizona Press, 1993.

Addams, Jane. *The Spirit of Youth and the City Streets.* New York: Macmillan, 1909.

Allen, Frederick Lewis. *Only Yesterday: An Informal History of the 1920s.* New York: Harper & Row, 1931.

Avila, Eric. *Popular Culture in the Age of White Flight: Fear and Fantasy in Suburban Los Angeles.* Berkeley: University of California Press, 2006.

Azzerad, Michael. *Our Band Could Be Your Life: Scenes from the American Indie Underground 1981–1991*. New York: Little, Brown, 2001.

Baldassare, Mark. *Trouble in Paradise: The Suburban Transformation in America*. New York: Columbia University Press, 1986.

———. ed. *Cities and Urban Living*. New York: Columbia University Press, 1983.

Blanchot, Maurice. "Everyday Speech." *Yale French Studies*, no. 73 (1987): 12–20.

Blumer, Herbert. *Movies and Conduct: A Payne Fund Study*. New York: Macmillan, 1933.

Blumin, Stuart. *The Emergence of the Middle Class: Social Experience in the American City, 1760–1900*. New York: Cambridge University Press, 1989.

Bottles, Scott L. *Los Angeles and the Automobile: The Making of the Modern City*. Berkeley: University of California Press, 1987.

Bourdieu, Pierre. *The Field of Cultural Production: Essays on Art and Literature*. New York: Columbia University Press, 1993.

Bourne, Randolph. "Transnational America." In *War and the Intellectuals: Essays by Randolph S. Bourne, 1915–1919*, edited by Carl Resek, 3–14. New York: Harper & Row, 1964.

———. *Untimely Papers*. Edited by James Oppenheim. New York: B. W. Huebsch, 1919.

———. *Youth and Life*. Boston: Houghton Mifflin, 1913.

Breines, Wini. *Young, White, and Miserable: Growing Up Female in the Fifties*. Boston: Beacon Press, 1992.

Certeau, Michel de. *The Practice of Everyday Life*. Berkeley: University of California Press, 1984.

Charters, W. W. *Motion Pictures and Youth: A Summary*. New York: Macmillan, 1933.

Clark, David L. "Improbable Los Angeles." In *Sunbelt Cities: Politics and Growth since World War II*, edited by Richard M. Bernard and Bradley R. Rice, 267–308. Austin: University of Texas Press, 1983.

Clarke, Gary. "Defending Ski-Jumpers: A Critique of Theories of Youth Subcultures." In *On Record: Rock, Pop, and the Written Word*, edited by Simon Frith and Andrew Goodwin, 81–96. New York: Pantheon, 1990.

Cocks, Jay. "Bringing Power to the People." *Time*, June 26, 1978. http://timeinc8-sd11.websys.aol.com/time/magazine/article/0,9171,916235-2,00.html.

Cole, Richard, and Richard Trubo. *Stairway to Heaven: Led Zeppelin Uncensored*. New York: Harper Collins, 1992.

Cote, James E., and Anton L. Allahar. *Generation on Hold: Coming of Age in the Late Twentieth Century*. New York: New York University Press, 1996.

Danielson, Michael N. *The Politics of Exclusion*. New York: Columbia University Press, 1976.

Dannen, Fredric. *Hit Men: Power Brokers and Fast Money inside the Music Business*. New York: Crown, 1990.

Davis, Mike. *City of Quartz: Excavating the Future in Los Angeles*. New York: Vintage, 1992.

Davis, Stephen. *Hammer of the Gods: The Led Zeppelin Saga.* New York: Penguin, 2001.

Denning, Michael. "The End of Mass Culture." In *Modernity and Mass Culture,* edited by James Naremore and Patrick Brantlinger, 253–68. Bloomington: Indiana University Press, 1991.

Douglas, Susan J. *Where the Girls Are: Growing Up Female with the Mass Media.* New York: Times Books, 1995.

Duncombe, Stephen. *Notes from Underground: Zines and the Politics of Alternative Culture.* London: Verso, 1997.

Eisen, Jonathan, David Fine, and Kim Eisen. *Unknown California.* New York: Doubleday, 1985.

Eliot, Marc. *Rockonomics: The Money behind the Music.* New York: Franklin Watts, 1989.

Engelhardt, Tom. *The End of Victory Culture: Cold War America and the Disillusioning of a Generation.* New York: Basic Books, 1995.

Ewen, Stuart. *PR! A Social History of Spin.* New York: Basic Books, 1996.

—— and Elizabeth Ewen. *Channels of Desire: Mass Images and the Shaping of American Consciousness.* 2nd ed. Minneapolis: University of Minnesota Press, 1992.

Fass, Paula S. *The Damned and the Beautiful: American Youth in the 1920s.* New York: Oxford University Press, 1977.

Fenichel, Otto. *The Psychoanalytic Theory of Neurosis.* New York: Norton, 1945.

Findlay, John M. *Magic Lands: Western Cityscapes and American Culture after 1940.* Berkeley: University of California Press, 1992.

Finnegan, William. *Cold New World: Growing Up in a Harder Country.* New York: Random House, 1998.

Fishman, Robert. *Bourgeois Utopias: The Rise and Fall of Suburbia.* New York: Basic Books, 1987.

Fogelson, Robert M. *The Fragmented Metropolis: Los Angeles, 1850–1930.* Cambridge, Mass.: Harvard University Press, 1967.

Frank, Thomas. *The Conquest of Cool: Business Culture, Counterculture, and the Rise of Hip Consumerism.* Chicago: University of Chicago Press, 1997.

Freeman, Richard B., and David A. Wise, eds. *The Youth Labor Market Problem: Its Nature, Causes and Consequences.* Chicago: University of Chicago Press, 1982.

Friedlander, Paul. *Rock and Roll: A Social History.* Boulder, Colo.: Westview Press, 1996.

Frith, Simon. "'The Magic That Can Set You Free': The Ideology of Folk and the Myth of the Rock Community." *Popular Music* 1 (1981): 159–68.

——. *Sound Effects: Youth, Leisure, and the Politics of Rock'n'Roll.* New York: Pantheon, 1981.

Gabler, Neal. *An Empire of Their Own: How the Jews Invented Hollywood.* New York: Doubleday, 1989.

Gilbert, James. *A Cycle of Outrage: America's Reaction to the Juvenile Delinquent in the*

1950s. New York: Oxford University Press, 1986.

Gillett, Charlie. *The Sound of the City: The Rise of Rock and Roll.* Cambridge, Mass.: Da Capo Press, 1996.

Giroux, Henry A. *Breaking in to the Movies: Film and the Culture of Politics.* Cambridge, Mass.: Blackwell, 2002.

Gitlin, Todd. *The Sixties: Years of Hope, Days of Rage.* New York: Bantam, 1987.

Goodman, Fred. *The Mansion on a Hill: Dylan, Young, Geffen, Springsteen and the Head-On Collision of Rock and Commerce.* New York: Crown, 1997.

Gottdiener, Mark D. "Social Planning and Metropolitan Growth." In *Handbook of Contemporary Urban Life,* edited by David Street, 494–518. San Francisco: Jossey-Bass, 1978.

Gottlieb, Joanne, and Gayle Wald. "Smells Like Teen Spirit: Riot Grrrls, Revolution and Women in Independent Rock." In *Microphone Fiends. Youth Music and Youth Culture,* edited by Andrew Ross and Tricia Rose, 250–74. New York: Routledge, 1994.

Grossberg, Lawrence. *We Gotta Get Out of This Place: Popular Conservatism and Postmodern Culture.* New York: Routledge, 1992.

Hall, Stuart. "Notes on Deconstructing 'the Popular.'" In *People's History and Socialist Theory,* edited by Raphael Samuel, 227–39. London: Routledge and Kegan Paul, 1981.

—— and Tony Jefferson, eds. *Resistance through Rituals: Youth Subcultures in Postwar Britain.* London: Hutchinson, 1976.

Harvey, David. *The Condition of Postmodernity: An Enquiry into the Origins of Cultural Change.* Cambridge, Mass.: Blackwell, 1989.

Higashi, Sumiko. *Cecil B. DeMille and American Culture: The Silent Era.* Berkeley: University of California Press, 1994.

Holt, Thomas C. "Marking: Race, Race-Making, and the Writing of History." *American Historical Review* 100, no. 1 (February 1995): 1–20.

Holtz, Geoffrey T. *Welcome to the Jungle: The Why behind "Generation X."* New York: St. Martin's, 1995.

Horkheimer, Max, and Theodor W. Adorno. *Dialectic of Enlightenment.* 1944. Reprint, New York: Herder and Herder, 1989.

Hoskyns, Barney. *Waiting for the Sun: Strange Days, Weird Scenes, and the Sound of Los Angeles.* New York: St. Martin's, 1996.

Jackson, Kenneth T. *The Crabgrass Frontier: The Suburbanization of the United States.* New York: Oxford University Press, 1985.

Jameson, Fredric. "Reification and Utopia in Mass Culture." *Social Text* 1 (Winter 1979): 130–48.

Jones, Landon Y. *Great Expectations: America and the Baby Boom Generation.* New York: Coward, McCann & Geoghegan, 1980.

Kasarda, John D. "Urbanization, Community, and the Metropolitan Problem." In *Handbook of Contemporary Urban Life,* edited by David Street, 27–57. San Francisco: Jossey-Bass, 1978.

Kett, Joseph F. *Rites of Passage: Adolescence in America, 1790 to the Present.* New York: Basic Books, 1977.

Kling, Rob, Spencer Olin, and Mark Poster, eds. *Postsuburban California: The Transformation of Orange County since World War II.* Berkeley: University of California Press, 1991.

Lamb, Karl A. *As Orange Goes: Twelve California Families and the Future of American Politics.* New York: Norton, 1974.

Larkin, Ralph. *Suburban Youth in Cultural Crisis.* New York: Oxford University Press, 1986.

Lasch, Christopher. *The Culture of Narcissism.* New York: Norton, 1979.

Lawrence, Tim. *Love Saves the Day: A History of American Dance Music Culture, 1970-1979.* Durham, N.C.: Duke University Press, 2003.

Lefebvre, Henri. *Everyday Life in the Modern World.* New Brunswick, N.J.: Transaction, 1984.

———. *Critique of Everyday Life.* New York: Verso, 1991.

Lifton, Robert J. "Protean Man." *Partisan Review* 35 (1968): 13–27.

Lipsitz, George. *Time Passages: Collective Memory and American Popular Culture.* Minneapolis: University of Minnesota Press, 1990.

Lo, Clarence Y. H. *Small Property versus Big Government: Social Origins of the Property Tax Revolt.* Berkeley: University of California Press, 1990.

Long, Larry H., and Paul C. Glick. "Family Patterns in Suburban Areas: Recent Trends." In *The Changing Face of the Suburbs,* edited by Barry Schwartz, 39–67. Chicago: University of Chicago Press, 1976.

Lott, Eric. *Love and Theft: Blackface Minstrelsy and the American Working Class.* New York: Oxford University Press, 1995.

Lowenthal, Leo. "The Triumph of Mass Idols." In Lowenthal, *Literature and Mass Culture,* 203–35. New Brunswick, N.J.: Transaction Books, 1984.

Lynd, Robert S., and Helen Merrell Lynd. *Middletown: A Study in Modern American Culture.* New York: Harcourt Brace Jovanovich, 1929.

Macdonald, Dwight. "A Theory of Mass Culture." In *Mass Culture: The Popular Arts in America,* edited by Bernard Rosenberg and David Manning White, 59–73. New York: Free Press, 1957.

Males, Mike A. *Scapegoat Generation: America's War on Adolescents.* Monroe, Maine: Common Courage Press, 1996.

Marcus, Greil. *Lipstick Traces: A Secret History of the Twentieth Century.* Cambridge, Mass.: Harvard University Press, 1989.

———. "Who Put the Bomp in the Bomp-de-Bomp?" In *Mass Culture Revisited,* edited by Bernard Rosenberg and David Manning White, 444–58. New York: Van Nostrand Reinhold, 1971.

May, Lary. *Screening Out the Past: The Birth of Mass Culture and the Motion Picture Industry.* New York: Oxford University Press, 1980.

McGirr, Lisa. *Suburban Warriors: The Origins of the New American Right.* Princeton,

N.J.: Princeton University Press, 2001.

McRobbie, Angela. *Postmodernism and Popular Culture*. New York: Routledge, 1994.

Meltzer, Richard. *L.A. is the Capital of Kansas*. New York: Random House, 1988.

———. *A Whore Just Like the Rest*. Cambridge, Mass.: Da Capo Press, 2000.

Miller, Mark Crispin. "Prime Time: Deride and Conquer." In *Watching Television: A Pantheon Guide to Popular Culture*, edited by Todd Gitlin, 183–228. New York: Pantheon, 1986.

Mills, C. Wright. *White Collar: The American Middle Classes*. New York: Oxford University Press, 1951.

Muller, Peter O. *Contemporary Suburban America*. Englewood Cliffs, N.J.: Prentice-Hall, 1981.

Naremore, James, and Patrick Brantlinger, eds. *Modernity and Mass Culture*. Bloomington: Indiana University Press, 1991.

Nasaw, David. *Children of the City: At Work and at Play*. New York: Oxford University Press, 1985.

———. *Going Out: The Rise and Fall of Public Amusements*. New York: Basic Books, 1994.

Nicolaides, Becky. *My Blue Heaven: Life and Politics in the Working-Class Suburbs of Los Angeles, 1920–1965*. Chicago: University of Chicago Press, 2002.

Offer, Daniel, Eric Ostrov, and Kenneth I. Howard. *The Adolescent: A Psychological Self-Portrait*. New York: Basic Books, 1981.

Osterman, Paul. *Getting Started: The Youth Labor Market*. Cambridge, Mass.: MIT Press, 1980.

Palladino, Grace. *Teenagers: An American History*. New York: Basic Books, 1996.

Peiss, Kathy. *Cheap Amusements: Working Women and Leisure in Turn-of-the-Century New York*. Philadelphia: Temple University Press, 1986.

Peterson, Richard A., and David G. Berger. "Cycles in Symbol Production: The Case of Popular Music." In *On Record: Rock, Pop, and the Written Word*, edited by Simon Frith and Andrew Goodwin, 140–59. New York: Pantheon, 1990.

Poster, Mark. "Narcissism or Liberation: The Affluent Middle-Class Family." In *Postsuburban California: The Transformation of Orange County since World War II*, edited by Rob Kling, Spencer Olin, and Mark Poster, 190–222. Berkeley: University of California Press, 1991.

Postman, Neil. *The Disappearance of Childhood*. New York: Delacorte, 1982.

Reisner, Marc. *Cadillac Desert: The American West and its Disappearing Water*. New York: Viking, 1986.

Reynolds, Simon, and Joy Press. *Sex Revolts: Gender, Rebellion, and Rock 'n' roll*. Cambridge, Mass.: Harvard University Press, 1996.

Riesman, David. *The Lonely Crowd: A Study of the Changing American Character*. New Haven, Conn.: Yale University Press, 1950.

Rosenberg, Bernard, and David Manning White, eds. *Mass Culture: The Popular Arts in America*. New York: Free Press, 1957.

———. *Mass Culture Revisited*. New York: Van Nostrand Reinhold, 1971.

Rowe, Peter G. *Making a Middle Landscape.* Cambridge, Mass.: MIT Press, 1991.

Schiesl, Martin J. "Designing the Model Community: The Irvine Company and Suburban Development, 1950–88." In *Postsuburban California: The Transformation of Orange County since World War II,* edited by Rob Kling, Spencer Olin, and Mark Poster, 55–91. Berkeley: University of California Press, 1991.

Scott, Allen J., and Edward W. Soja, eds. *The City: Los Angeles and Urban Theory at the End of the Twentieth Century.* Berkeley: University of California Press, 1996.

Shank, Barry. *Dissonant Identities: The Rock 'n' roll Scene in Austin, Texas.* Hanover, N.H.: Wesleyan University Press, 1994.

Soja, Edward W. "Inside Exopolis: Scenes from Orange County." In *Variations on a Theme Park: The New American City and the End of Public Space,* edited by Michael Sorkin, 94–122. New York: Noonday, 1992.

———. "Los Angeles, 1965–1992: From Crisis-Generated Restructuring to Restructuring-Generated Crisis." In *The City: Los Angeles and Urban Theory at the End of the Twentieth Century,* edited by Allen J. Scott and Edward W. Soja, 426–62. Berkeley: University of California Press, 1996.

Spigel, Lynn. *Make Room for TV: Television and the Family Ideal in Postwar America.* Chicago: University of Chicago Press, 1992.

Stansell, Christine. *City of Women: Sex and Class in New York, 1789–1860.* Urbana: University of Illinois Press, 1987.

Street, David. ed. *Handbook of Contemporary Urban Life.* San Francisco: Jossey-Bass, 1978.

Teaford, Jon C. *Post-Suburbia: Government and Politics in the Edge Cities.* Baltimore: Johns Hopkins University Press, 1997.

Thornton, Sarah. *Club Cultures: Music, Media, and Subcultural Capital.* Hanover, N.H.: Wesleyan University Press, 1996.

Tocqueville, Alexis de. *Democracy in America.* Abridged ed. New York: New American Library, 1956.

Venkatesh, Alladi. "Changing Consumption Patterns." In *Postsuburban California: The Transformation of Orange County since World War II,* edited by Rob Kling, Spencer Olin, and Mark Poster, 142–64. Berkeley: University of California Press, 1991.

Viehe, Fred W. "Black Gold Suburbs: The Influence of the Extractive Industry on the Suburbanization of Los Angeles." *Journal of Urban History* 8 (November 1981): 3–26.

Wachs, Martin. "The Evolution of Transportation Policy in Los Angeles." In *The City: Los Angeles and Urban Theory at the End of the Twentieth Century,* edited by Allen J. Scott and Edward W. Soja, 106–59. Berkeley: University of California Press, 1996.

Waldinger, Robert, and Mehdi Bozorgmehr, eds. *Ethnic Los Angeles.* New York: Russell Sage Foundation, 1996.

White, Merry. *The Material Child: Coming of Age in Japan and America.* New York: Free Press, 1993.

Wicke, Peter. *Rock Music: Culture, Aesthetics and Sociology.* Cambridge, UK: Cambridge University Press, 1990.

Willard, Michael. "Seance, Tricknowlogy, Skateboarding, and the Space of Youth." In *Generations of Youth: Youth Cultures and History in Twentieth Century America,* edited by Joe Austin and Michael Willard, 327–46. New York: New York University Press, 1998.

Wilson, Hugh A. "The Family in Suburbia: From Tradition to Pluralism." In *Suburbia Re-examined,* edited by Barbara M. Kelly, 85–93. New York: Greenwood, 1979.

Zines, Magazines, and Newspapers

BAM

Bomp! (Los Angeles)

Creem

Damage (San Francisco)

Details

Flipside (Whittier)

Forget It! (San Jose)

Generation Magazine (Los Angeles)

Generation X (North Hollywood)

Goldmine

The L.A. Beat (Long Beach)

Lobotomy (Los Angeles)

Los Angeles Times

Maximum Rocknroll (San Francisco)

Musician

Outcry (South Pasadena)

Panic (Los Angeles)

People

Punk (New York)

Quasi-Substitute (La Mesa)

Record Review (Los Angeles)

Ripper (San Jose)

Rockin' in the Fourth Estate (New York)

Rolling Stone

Search and Destroy (San Francisco)

Slash (Los Angeles)

Wasteland (Los Angeles)

Films and Television Shows

CHiPs. "Battle of the Bands," by Larry Mollin, directed by Barry Crane, originally aired January 31, 1982.

Class of 1984. Directed by Mark Lester. United Film Distribution, 1981.

The Decline of Western Civilization. Directed by Penelope Spheeris. Spheeris Films, 1981.

Donahue. "Parents of Punkers," Transcript #01212, Episode #760, aired January 21, 1982.

Hunter. "Death Machine," by Tom Lazarus, directed by Kim Manners, originally aired March 11, 1986.

Quincy M.E. "Next Stop, Nowhere," by Sam Egan, directed by Ray Danton, originally aired December 1, 1982.

Repo Man. Directed by Alex Cox. Universal Pictures, 1984.

Return of the Living Dead. Directed by Dan O'Bannon. Orion Pictures, 1984.

Road Warrior. Directed by George Miller. Warner Brothers Pictures, 1981.

Suburbia. Directed by Penelope Spheeris. New World Pictures, 1983.

Liner Notes

Coley, Byron. Liner notes to rerelease of Flesh Eaters, *No Questions Asked*. Chicago: Atavistic Records, 2004.

Gehman, Pleasant. Liner notes to Germs, *(MIA): The Complete Anthology*. Los Angeles: Slash Records, 1993.

Geza X. Liner notes to Germs, *Rock N' Rule: Live at the Masque Reunion Christmas 1979*. Los Angeles: XES Records, 1986.

Liner notes to Middle Class, *a blueprint for joy 1978–1980*. Los Angeles: Velvetone Records, 1995.

Liner notes to Various Artists, *Someone Got Their Head Kicked In!* Los Angeles: BYO Records, 1982.

Liner notes to Various Artists, *Someone's Gonna Get Their Head to Believe in Something*. Los Angeles: BYO Records, 1992.

Mullen, Brendan. Liner notes to Various Artists, *Live from the Masque 1978*. Whittier: Flipside Records, 1994.

Pavitt, Bruce. Liner notes to Various Artists, *American Youth Report*. Los Angeles: Invasion Records, a division of Bomp Records, 1982.

Spot. Liner notes to Black Flag, *Everything Went Black*. Los Angeles: SST Records, 1983.

Interviews

John Platt, personal conversation, January 15, 1994

Matt Bokovoy, December 29, 1994

Falling James, January 11, 1995

Jon Lalanne, January 12, 1995

Stephen Shea, January 12, 1995

Katie Golden, January 12, 1995

Raymond Bridgers, January 13, 1995

Pooch, January 13, 1995

Tony Reflex, July 12, 1995

Blaze James, October 3, 1995

Tony Reflex, October 3, 1995

Al Flipside, October 3, 1995

Brendan Mullen, October 8, 1995

Tony Reflex, May 10, 1997

Kristine McKenna, October 14, 1997

Tito Larriva, September 13, 1998

Acknowledgments

What would D. Boon Do?

David Rees, 2005

I owe many people large debts for their help in getting me through this book. For help with research, my thanks to Randy Metz, Eddie Egan, Al Flipside, Pooch, Tony Reflex-Cadena-Brandenburg, and the late Brendan Mullen. Al was particularly generous in opening up his own personal archives to me, and Tony put me in touch with anyone I needed to know, becoming a valued source of support.

Thanks to friends and colleagues who have stimulated my thinking and given me support over the years: Brian Gamble, David Jacobson, Jack Donovan, Paula Stamatis, Stephen Duncombe, Janet Donofrio, David Rieth, Larry Fessenden, Diana Linden, Leslie Horowitz, Eva Moskowitz, Simon Middleton, Jon Sterngass, Lisa Robb, Charles Malone, Stephen Shea, Karen Sotiropoluous, Nancy K. Miller, Luc Menand, Sheila Mylan, and Roberta Baldwin. My thanks and apologies to those I have forgotten.

Stuart Ewen gave me early encouragement to pursue this project and a helpful reading of the first draft, which has made the book much better. For thoughtful readings of excerpts and drafts, thanks especially to Sean McCann and Celia Bland. Neil Baldwin provided support at several key moments.

Carol Berkin taught me how to be a historian and secured me as a lifelong devotee both of her personally and of the thick, gooey richness of history. David Nasaw called upon all his patience and wisdom to guide me through my dissertation, which became the basis for this book.

Berta Bilezikjian taught me the first pieces of being a historian. What a marvel she was, Miss Billings, as we called her, who taught me to love words from the past and to argue a point. Miss Billings, I still have your *Problems in American History* series that you loaned to my sister; you can claim them any time, or I will keep and cherish them. D. Carroll Joynes indulged my fascination with Foucault, secured me a position in Eric Hobsbawm's grad classes, mentored me through my B.A., and befriended me for the duration.

At William Paterson University I have been fortunate to have the strong support of my colleagues in the History Department, especially Evelyn Gonzalez, who has championed me since the day I arrived; Dean Isabel Tirado, who kicked in some cash from her secret stash and offered me the opportunity to share my work with colleagues at the wonderful HSS research forums; and Nina Jemmott, Steve Hahn, Ed Weil, and the folks at the Provost's Office, whose ART I was supposed to use for other work but instead used to concoct yet one more draft. I don't think I owe any specific obligations to the librarians at WPU for this project, but Anne Ciliberti runs a clean machine, and Richard Kearney is an excellent historian himself and a great help.

This manuscript has been blessed with several editors, none of whom should be blamed for failing to make it better than it is. Brendan O'Malley championed the book fiercely. Long before joining the University of Oklahoma Press, Matt Bokovoy provided me with the most trenchant and helpful readings. Matt came to see my first academic presentation on punk sometime in the last century, and he has remained a friend ever since. After he moved on, Kirk Bjornsgaard, Julie Shilling, Jane Lyle, Phil Bansal, and Steven Baker all helped me ready the manuscript for publication. Ronn Spencer, Gary Panter, Jenny Lens, and John Emerson were kind enough to allow me to share their extraordinary visual art with my readers.

I am so grateful to so many people who have done me favors great and small and who have entered my life at just the right moment. Thanks particularly to Christine Kelly, Roger Sedarat, Naomi Serlen, and to the folks at Glen Ridge Taekwon-do, especially Master James Marr and Patricia Papera.

Jacobus Schmidt has never lost faith in me, nor I in him—despite all evidence. I will never be able to express the depth of my gratitude and love. My siblings, Jackie, Sheila, Jennifer, and John, and my father, James, have rescued me more than once and more than I deserve. Rory is a budding skate-rat grommet who loves his Green Day and Dropkick Murphys, but will still give me a kiss any time I ask. Sinéad is the coolest person I know. Among her many talents, her ability to absorb, assimilate, and assess pop culture continually amazes me. My most cherished moments are taking her to shows by Iggy and the Stooges (with the inimitable Mike Watt on bass), Gang of Four, Heartless Bastards, PJ Harvey, Roky Erickson, and more. Even though she doesn't need me to get her into clubs so much anymore, she will still accept the occasional free ticket.

Finally, this book would not exist without Deirdre. I owe her a lifetime of gratitude for twenty extraordinary years.

Index

environment, 104; rejection of by the Middle Class, 106; and youth culture, 49–50

Controllers, 33, 91, 132

Conversion, instant, 66

Cook, Paul (Sex Pistols), 43

"Cops are out" (Battalion of Saints), 115

Corporate capitalism, 77

Costa Mesa, Calif., 95

Costello, Elvis, 12, 79

Country/folk rock, 53

C.P.O. Sharkey (TV show), 77–78

Crash, Darby (Germs), 83–84, 85, 135. *See also* Beahm, Jan Paul; Pyn, Bobby

Crass, 84, 134

Crawdaddy! (zine), 54–55

"Creatures" (Adolescents), 133

Creem (magazine), 12, 75

Crime, 42

Crowd (band), 121

Crowe, Cameron, 99–100

Crucifix, 13

Cuckoo's Nest, 95

"Daddy's gone mad" (Legal Weapon), 102

Damaged (Black Flag), 95

Damned, The: at Bomp Records store in April 1977, 23, 54; first English punk band on vinyl, 23; return of, 81–82; theatricality of, 36

Dance floor, hardcore shows, 123

Dangerous (Jackson), 135

Darby Crash Band, 85

Day-Glo set, 61, 65, 82, 95, 121

Deadbeats, 34

Dead Kennedys, 13, 42, 103, 131

Decline of Western Civilization, The (film) (Spheeris), 83, 100–101, 121

DeMille, Cecile B., 31

Denny, John (Weirdos), 34

Deren, Maya, 133

Descendents, 96, 102, 106, 118, 134

"Destroy All Music" (Weirdos), 30

Detroit, Randy, 1, 45, 58

Diana and Michelle (*The Panic*), 58

Dickies, 34, 71–72, 77–78

Dils (later Rank and File), 21, 26, 34, 42, 86, 90, 133

Disco, 30, 53, 138n25. *See also* Rodney's English Disco

Divine Horseman, 133

DIY (do-it-yourself) ethos: all fans as active participants, 53; as alternative way of realizing ideals of youth culture, 57; barely listenable "music" produced by, 96; and Bomp! as model of, 54–55; continuing today, 134; definition of, 53; and "Forming," 59–60; and postsuburban youth, 99; and Shaw, 70; and underground culture, 56; and vinyl production, 77

DOA, 118

Doe, John (X), 63–64, 65, 77

Dogs (Radio Free Hollywood), 20, 61

Do-it-yourself ethos (DIY). *See* DIY (do-it-yourself) ethos

Doom, Lorna (Terry Ryan), 23

Doors, 21, 26

"Do the Uganda" (Controllers), 132

"Do They Owe Us a Living?" (Crass), 134

Downey, Calif., 133

Dream Syndicate, 134

Dred Scott (band), 132

Dressing punk: and Black Flag, 94; and DIY ethos, 53; "glitter kids," 17; and hardcore punk, 84, 96; and the LAPD, 109; and the Middle Class, 91, 93; mixed with New Wave, 68; and punk identity, 1, 57, 67, 79–80

Dukowski, Chuck (Black Flag), 94, 109, 110

Du Plenty, Tomata (Screamers), 61, 102

Dylan, Bob, 14

"Gimmie Shock Treatment" (Ramones), 14

Ginn, Greg (Black Flag), 94, 96

Go-Gos, 68, 81, 107

Good Charlotte, 135

Graham, Bill, 42, 43, 44, 139n7

Grateful Dead, 14, 54

Great Depression and youth, 48

Green Day, 96

Grisham, Jack (Vicious Circle; later T.S.O.L.), 121–22

Haight-Ashbury (1967), 54, 55

Hair: and flappers, 48; instant conversion, 66; long, 18, 67, 73, 74; modified for punk, 12; Mohawks, 1; short, 66; spiked, 1, 62

Hardcore California (Lee), 26

Hardcore punk: anti-Reagan message of, 103–105; ascendancy of in suburbs, 134; attitude toward family life, 103; and the dance floor, 123; do-it-yourself anarchism, 100; emergence of, 98; exclusivity of, 96; and the family in postsuburbia, 100–106; and gangs, 123; and "killing the father," 104; as male music, 132; mothers absent from lyrics, 106; and "no rules," 122, 149n52; and philosophy of rage, 122; and politics of, 4, 118; popularity of, 120–21; protest songs of, 103; as pursuit of reality, 126; race a minor theme, 131; and rejection of interaction with dominant culture, 53; transition of punk to, 99; as white music, 131.

Hardcore punk and violence, 110–11, 146n10; attractive to new breed of punk, 130; at Baces Hall, 120–21; and *Clockwork Orange* as model for, 125; conflict within hardcore over violence, 124–25; at core of new beach scene, 120–22; debate over meaning of, 123–24; directed both within and without, 126; endemic to the scene, 130; at Hideaway

Club in 1980, 118–19; and rise of postsuburban punk, 112; scene defined by violence, 125; at Whisky a Go-Go in 1980, 119–20

HBs (Huntington Beach punks), 121–24, 128

Hebdige, Dick, 86

Hector (Penalosa of the Zeros), 91, 133

Hell, Richard, 15, 46

"Hepcats from Hell" (radio show), 73

Hermosa Bath House, 93

Hermosa Beach, Calif., 82, 90, 91, 93, 94, 102, 128

Heroin, 78–79, 97

Hideaway Club show, 118–19

Hilburn, Robert, 62, 63

Hippies, instant conversion of, 66

"History Lesson Part 2" (Minutemen), 136

Hollywood Center Building, 31, 138n31

Hollywood 50 (in-group of punks), 38, 72

Hollywood Punk Palace, 21

Hollywood punk scene: and beginning of punk, 2–3; and Bomp Records Store, 21–22, 38; disavowal of new wave, 98; and Hollywood 50 (Fifty), 38; Hollywood Punk Palace, 21; loss of dominance, 97; Radio Free Hollywood, 20; rejection of suburban punks, 91–92

"Home Is Where We Hide" (Middle Class), 102

Homeowner self-defense in Southern California, 116, 148n36

Homophobia, 133

Housing development in Southern California, 88–89, 100–101, 116, 148n38

Houston, Penelope (Avengers), 45

Howlin' Wolf, 20

Hudley (*Flipside*), 124

Huntington Beach, Calif., 90, 121–24

Identity as punks: appearance of, 1; and connection to music and scenes,

136; as full-time punks, 37–38; and postsuburbia, 75. *See also* Art-damaged punks; Canterbury Apartments; Dressing punk; Hair; Masque (punk club)

"Idi Amin" (Black Randy and the Metrosquad), 131–32

"I hate" (Rotten's T-shirt), 15

"I Hate the Rich" (Dils), 86

Insiders vs. outsiders, 72

"Institutionalized" (Suicidal Tendencies), 105–106

Interstate Highway Act of 1956, 89

Irrigation, 87, 144n8

Irvine Company (Orange County), 113

"I've Had It" (Black Flag), 122

"I Wanna Be Sedated" (Ramones), 15

"I Wanna Be Your Dog" (Iggy Pop), 18

I Wanna Be Your Dog (zine), 58

Jackson, Joe, 79

Jackson, Michael, 135

Jefferson Airplane, 54

Jett, Joan, 20, 102

Joanne K., 58

John Birch Society, 116, 147n35

Joke-punk songs, 77

Joke Records (Star), 91

Jones, Davy, 16

Joplin, Janis, 54

Karla "Mad Dog" (Controllers), 132

Kat (Legal Weapon), 102

Kickboy Face. *See* Bessy, Claude

"Kids of the Black Hole" (Adolescents), 102

Kinman, Chip (Dils), 26, 42

Kinman, Tony (Dils), 42

Klan, 95

Klaxophone, 36

Knack, 80

KROQ (radio station), 20–21

"L.A. Girl" (Adolescents), 133

"La-la-las won't kill you" (Shaw), 69

La Mirada Punks, 116

La Mirada Stoners (nonpunks), 116

L.A. punk scene: ambivalence toward dominant culture, 53; April 16, 1977, performance, 25; artistic rebellion of, 26; attracted to punk by theatricality, 57; conversion experience of, 66; The Damned's arrival in April 1977, 26; and Elks Lodge Massacre, 107–109; exclusiveness of, 37–39; influences embraced by, 36; maturing of scene, 61; mocks decline of Hollywood grandeur, 34–36; music secondary to performance, 34, 57; vs. New Wave, 71; and power pop, 67–70; punks as "art damaged," 39; redefining, 66–67; as response to the city, 87; response to wider cultural influences of, 27; and the scene, 74–79; show that became catalyst for punk in, 27; and subculture ideologies, 37. *See also* Art-damaged punks; Canterbury Apartments; Identity as punks; Masque (punk club)

Larchmont Hall, 76, 91

Larriva, Tito (Plugz), 59, 107–108, 134

Lasch, Christopher, 30

Laser and the Motels (Radio Free Hollywood), 20

Last, 69

Latin influences, 134

Led Zeppelin, 11, 12, 16

Lee, Craig, 26, 36, 37–38, 72

Legal Weapon, 102

Licorice Pizza record store, 12

"Live fast/Die young" (Circle Jerks), 122

Lobotomy: the brainless magazine (zine), 45, 58

Long Beach, Calif., 95

Lopez, Robert (Zeros; El Vez), 133

"Los Angeles" (X), 132

Los Angeles (X album on Slash Records), 98

Los Angeles County schools, integration of, 118

Los Angeles history: and DIY ethos of postsurburbia, 99; downtown becomes "Fortress L.A.," 101; and Elks Lodge Massacre, 107–109; and Masque's closing, 98; and property tax increases, 117; and Proposition 13, 118; and right-wing Otis Chandler dynasty, 116; and school integration, 118

Los Angeles in the seventies: author's introduction to punk, 11–12; and the automobile, 87; conservative politics of, 116; cultural traditions of, 10; factors leading to postsuburbia, 88–89; and influential pioneers, 16; and punk war against music business, 28–30; show that became catalyst for punk in, 23; violence encountered by new arrivals, 10; youth culture of, 9; youths' motivation for going to, 9–10

Los Angeles Times: in defense of punks, 109; on Elks Lodge benefit shows, 61–62; Otis-Chandler dynasty, 116; positive reviews of punk in, 62; on punk violence, 110–11, 146n10; X as the band of the year, 98

Los Lobos, 134

Love, 21

Lowe, Nick, 12

Lynyrd Skynyrd, 11

Mabuhay Gardens restaurant (San Francisco), 42

"Macho Man," 13

Madame Wongs, 78

Mad Society, 118

Male domination of punk, 132–33

Malls, shopping, 99, 100–101

Marcus, Greil, 63

Masque (punk club), 34; and Bobby Pyn, 33; closings of, 97, 98; Elks Club benefit concert for, 61, 79, 142n1; faithful audience of, 37; and female punk cliques, 121; openings of, 31–32, 78; rejection of the Middle Class by, 91

Mass culture: ambivalence of *Slash* toward, 70; coming-of-age youth feel cheated of connection with, 51–52; coming-of-age youth missed connection with, 46–48; dramatic changes in seventies, 2–3; and emergence of postsuburbia, 90–93; ideologies failed to unify young people, 4; and postsuburban youth, 98–99; and postwar era, 49–50; rejection of, 136; rock 'n' roll as escape in fifties, 50–51; and standardizing effects of film, 48–49; and underground culture, 56–57. *See also* Youth and mass culture

Maximum Rocknroll (zine), 135

"Mayday 1977" (Kickboy Face), 28

MC5, 13

McGuire, Barry, 50, 72

McKenna, Kristine, review of L.A. punk, 62, 66

McLaren, Malcolm (Sex Pistols), 14, 43–44, 61, 134

McNeil, Legs (*Punk* magazine), 139n7

Meat Puppets, 135

Meltzer, Richard (Vom), 42–43, 73

Metaconsumers, defined, 99

Metrosquad, 13, 34, 131–32

Michelle and Diana (*The Panic*), 58

Middle Class, the: formation of, 91; "Home Is Where We Hide," 102; at Larchmont Hall, 91; and Mullen, 91; "Out of Vogue," 91, 105; positive review by *Slash*, 92; of suburbia, 3

Millikan High School (Long Beach), 95

Milo (Descendents), 102

Minor Threat, 136

Minutemen, 118, 126

Misogyny, 133

Modern Lovers, 13

Modern Warfare, 96

Mohawks, 1

Ramones: appeal to working class, 2; attention on English tour, 14; author's impression of, 12; cartoonish thug persona of, 14; and outsiders, 76; revolutionary sound of, 13; at Whisky a Go-Go, 11; worldwide impact of, 14

Raw Power (Iggy Pop album), 18

Raw Power (zine), 58

Reagan, Ronald, 103–105, 129, 134

Real estate industry, and L.A., 87

"Real punk," 37–38

Red Cross, 95

Redondo Beach, Calif., 95

Reid, Jamie, 86

Repo Man (film), 103, 111

Return of the Living Dead (film), 111

Rickles, Don, 77–78

"Rip It Up" (Adolescents), 124–25

Road building vs. mass transit in L.A., 88

Road Warrior (film), 111

Rockabilly, 133

Rock contrasted to pop, 39

Rocket from the Tombs, 13

Rock 'n' roll: and early punk rock, 76; and Fancher and Shaw, 56; now Rock, 14, 30; as outlet for artistic expression, 57; power to unify youth culture, 55–56; relationship to punk, 68; return to, 14; status in 1970 to 1972, 55; threatened by punk, 2

"Rock N Roll Nigger" (Smith), 131

Rock stars from Woodstock era, 18

"Rodney on the Roq," 59

Rodney's English Disco, 16–18, 20

Rolling Stone magazine (Wenner), 42, 55

Rollins, Henry (Black Flag), tour diary of, 126–27

Roman, Cliff (Weirdos), 21

Ronstadt, Linda, 10, 76

Rotten, Johnny (Sex Pistols; Public Image Ltd.), 15, 43–44, 45, 133, 134

Runaways, 20

Ruthenberg, George (later Pat Smear), 20, 23. *See also* Smear, Pat

Saccharine Trust, 118, 132

Samiof, Steve, 27, 32

San Diego, Calif., 97

San Fernando Valley, Calif., 97

San Francisco Mime Troupe, 42

San Francisco punk scene: and dialogue with L.A. punk, 26; growth of, 42; left-wing politics of Bay Area, 136; media blitz of Bay Area, 112, 146n16; publication of first zine, 54; and Winterland show (1978), 41–46. *See also* Dead Kennedys

Santa Ana, Calif., 91

Santa Barbara, Calif., 97

Santa Monica, Calif., 97

Santa Monica Civic Auditorium, 96

Savio, Mario, 50

Scabies, Rat (The Damned), 25, 81–82, 143n39

Schulberg, Budd, 9

Screamers, 23, 31, 33, 34, 36, 57

"Search and Destroy" (Iggy Pop), 18

Search & Destroy (zine), 44

Self-mutilation of punks, 126

Seventies culture, 69

"Sex Boy" (Germs), 59–60

Sex on Kings Road, 14

Sex Pistols: Cliff Roman remembers, 21; formation of, 2; impact of, 64–65; influence of, 63–64; and McLaren, 14, 61; and outsiders, 76; tour of United States in 1978, 41–42; and Winterland show (1978), 41–46, 70

Sgt. Pepper's Lonely Hearts Club Band (Beatles album), 30

Shaw, Greg: Bomp Records formed by, 56–57; and debate with Mullen, 68–69; editor of zines, 54–55, 132; opposition to music industry, 99–100; owner of Bomp Records store, 21–22, 68; power pop promotion denied by, 69–70; promotion of punk by, 69, 142n17; survival of in the scene, 75

Shopping malls, 99, 100–101

Short Ice, 21

Shreader (*Rag in Chains*), 97, 112

Sioux, Siouxsie (London), 14, 131, 132

SIR Studios soundstage, 21

Skanking (slam dancing), 83, 143n1

Skate punk culture, 115, 147n29

Skinhead look, 131

"Skinhead Manor," 102

Skrews, 95, 120

Skulls, 31, 33, 61

Slam dancing, 111

Slash (zine), 12; on ambivalence toward newcomers, 66; creation of, 27–28; final issue of, 98; manifesto for punk revolution, 30–31; on opposition to New Wave, 80; positive review of suburban bands, 92; positive reviews of X, 62–63; professionally printed, 58; and punk potty photos, 61; record label established by, 59; and Skulls performance for staff of, 32; as voice of punk, 66–67; voice of punk's two positions, 57–58; on Winterland show controversy, 45, 140n15. *See also* Bessy, Claude

Slashers, 95, 122

Slash Records, 98

Slaughter and the Dogs, 14

Slush (zine), 98

Smear, Pat (George Ruthenberg), 20, 23, 121. *See also* Ruthenberg, George

Smith, Patti, 80, 86, 131, 132, 135

Sniffin Glue (zine), 53

So Cal punk, 1, 132

Social Distortion, 95, 102

"Sophistifuck and The Revlon Spam Queens" (fake band), 20

"So This Is War, Eh?" (Kickboy Face), 28, 30

Sound Effects (Frith), 86–87

South Pasadena, Calif., 97

Space, struggles over, 113

Spheeris, Penelope, 83, 100–101

Spot (Black Flag), 93, 123

SST Records (Black Flag), 91, 94, 135

Starwood, 78, 79, 81

Stiph, Steve (*Outcry*), on HB violence, 124

Stooges, 13

Straight edge, 136

Students for a Democratic Society, 50

Styrene, Poly, 132

Subculture (Hebdige), 86

Subculture: and authenticity, 39–40; being punk as full-time endeavor, 38; blurring of line between dominant culture and, 109; cross-pollination of in DIY tradition, 134; decentralization of postsuburbia mirrored by punk, 114; development of mass, 135–36; and distinction between insiders and outsiders, 37; of London punk, 2; as minor in United States until *Nevermind* album, 16; punk as working-class youth, 86; results of studies on punk rock, 86–87; *Slash* as line between dominant culture and the, 65–66; *Slash* editorial was catalyst in L.A. for punk, 30; violence as endemic to scene, 125–26, 128–30; of youth violence, 127–30

Suburban bands, 97

"Suburban Home" (Descendents), 106

Suburban punk: changes in seventies, 2; homegrown record labels of, 91–92; new punk bands emerging, 95; and punk's exclusivity, 96–97; "real punk," 37–38. *See also* Black Flag; Middle Class, the

Suburbia (film) (Spheeris), 101–102, 103, 111

Subway Sect, 14

Yes, 12

Youth and mass culture: and appeal of
New Left, 50–51; and assimilation
of immigrant youth, 47–48; and
consumerism, 49–50; and continual
"youth problem" of society, 47; and folk
culture threatened by mass culture,
48; as identical, 51; postwar era and,
1–2, 49–50; and protest songs of the
sixties, 50; and rock 'n' roll in 1950s, 50;
and spread of fifties youth culture, 49,
140n27; and standardization of mass
culture, 49; and women and cultural
changes, 48, 140n22. *See also* Mass
culture

Youth Brigade ("Boys in the Brigade"), 116

Youth culture: ascendancy of at end of
sixties, 51, 98; changes in seventies, 2, ·
51, 98–99, 145n43; end of, 51–53; and
music industry, 52–53; in postsuburbia,
98–100; power of rock 'n' roll to unify,
55, 57; and prolonged adolescence of
baby boomers, 51–52, 141n39; rock's
capacity to make youth feel something,
26, 99, 121; and shopping malls, 99,
100–101; violence through the decades,
129; youth as metaconsumers, 99

Zandra, 58
Zebest, Jade, 58
Zeros, 23, 34, 107
Zines (fanzines), proliferation of, 58
Zippers, 21
Zolar-X, 9, 21
Zoom, Billy (X), 63